# HOW LONG DOES IT HURT?

# How Long Does It Hurt?

A GUIDE TO
RECOVERING
FROM INCEST AND
SEXUAL ABUSE
FOR TEENAGERS,
THEIR FRIENDS,
AND THEIR FAMILIES

CYNTHIA L. MATHER

With Kristina E. Debye, LCSW-C, ACSW, DCSW

Illustrations by Judy Wood

Foreword by Eliana Gil, PH.D.

JOSSEY-BASS PUBLISHERS • SAN FRANCISCO

Manufactured in the United States of America. Nearly all Jossey-Bass books and jackets are printed on recycled paper that contains at least 50 percent recycled waste, including 10 percent postconsumer

Substantial discounts on bulk quantities of Jossey-Bass books are available to corporations, professional associations, and other organizations. For details and discount information, contact the special sales department at Jossey-Bass Inc., Pubishers. (415) 433-1740; Fax (415) 433-0499.

waste. Many of our materials are also printed with vegetable-based ink; during the printing process these inks emit fewer volatile organic compounds (VOCs) than petroleum-based inks. VOCs contribute to the formation of smog.

### Library of Congress Cataloging-in-Publication Data

Mather, Cynthia L. (Cynthia Lynn), date.
    How long does it hurt? : a guide to recovering from incest and sexual
abuse for teenagers, their friends, and their families /
Cynthia L. Mather with Kristina E. Debye ; illustrations by Judy
Wood ; foreword by Eliana Gil. — 1st ed.
      p. cm. — (The Jossey-Bass social and behavioral science
    series)
    Includes index.
    ISBN 1-55542-674-3
    1. Incest victims—Rehabilitation—United States. 2. Sexually
abused teenagers—Rehabilitation—United States. 3. Incest—United
States—Psychological aspects. I. Debye, Kristina E. II. Title.
III. Series: Jossey-Bass social and behavioral science series.
HV6570.7.M37 1994
362.7'68'0973—dc20

94-12536
CIP

FIRST EDITION
PB Printing   10 9 8 7 6 5 4 3 2 1       *Code* 9475

Dedicated to

**Kristen**

and all my younger

brothers and sisters who are hurting

In loving memory of:

**Richard W. Wood, Jr.**
1931-1994

**Elizabeth C. Darwe**
1909-1994

# Contents

## PART FOUR: THINGS TO KNOW

# Thank You

**I** WISH I COULD take full credit for writing this book. I can't. Too many people in my life have been a part of this labor for me to say, "I did it myself."

I must first give thanks to God, who has poured His love and healing all over the wounds of my life. To do that, He has used the people I have listed below and others who are no longer a part of my life but who have left their fingerprints all over it. There were many times during the writing of this work that I knew I was simply an instrument. I am grateful and humbled that He has used me in this way.

My fondest thanks to the "small group"—Jim and Ann, Don and Donna, Carl and Susan, Dick and Judy, Ham and Joann, Jim and Audrey—who listened with so much love as I told them my story and who have in so many different ways supported me through this work.

My gratitude to Kris Debye, my collaborator, who was the first professional to offer me encouragement and later the use of her experience and name. This book is a better book because of Kris's involvement. If there are any errors, I must claim them. Kris did her best in dealing with my strong will.

To the Reverend Faith Jongewaard, my thanks for the garden discussions about forgiveness. To the Reverend Carl vom Eigen, my thanks for teaching me a new idea of reconciliation. To Jennifer Nabet, thanks for pointing me in the right direction. To Dr. Audrey Gift, thanks for getting me started. To Jim Mather, thanks for giving life to the characters.

Every writer needs a push now and then. My "pushy" force was Susan Euker—she kept opening doors and pushing me through. Thank you, Susan.

In my life, I have known love that is a weapon and love that bears a price tag. But I have also been blessed with knowing love that is unconditional. For that I am grateful to the three most important men in my life: my husband, Dennis, and my sons, Jim and Chris. Without their support and encouragement, this book would not be. Thank you, guys, for understanding about the missed soccer games, the unwashed clothes, and the uncooked meals. And to Denny, "thank you" will never cover what I feel for your steadfastness and love in my life.

Finally, my deepest thanks to the many kids who talked to me, wrote to me, shared with me. Your candor has been a gift, your encouragement an inspiration, your need a reason to keep going. Ultimately this book belongs to you.

C.L.M.

# Foreword

THIS IS A book for a special group of teenagers—young people who are facing all the usual problems of growing up but who are also unique in a different way: they are struggling to survive incest or sexual abuse.

If you are reading this, something in the title attracted your attention. You may be in a bad situation yourself right now. You may have been hurt when you were younger, or have a friend or relative who has been hurt. You may feel caught between wanting to think about it and wanting to forget. You probably have lots of questions on your mind, and this book can help you sort through some of the possible answers.

I say answers because there is no one way to think about, feel about, or work out incest or child sexual abuse. Just as each person is unique, so the solutions to each person's problems are also unique. That is one of the ways this book succeeds so well. It doesn't try to "fix things" for you. It helps you look at, and think about, lots of concerns. What works for you may not work for anyone else.

Incest and sexual abuse are very complicated problems. Incest occurs when an adult (or an older kid) in your family, or someone acting in the role of a family member, like a stepparent, does (or tries to do) something sexual with you. At first you may wonder if you did something wrong, or if you are imagining things. Later, you may still wonder if you are being bad in some way that causes the incest, or what to do to make it stop. But the fact that you love the person who is doing something wrong makes it more difficult for you to know what to do next.

In cases of sexual abuse that don't involve family members, you may still feel caught in a bind. You may trust, like, and want to spend time with the adult, and yet now you feel confused or frightened about this person's sexual behavior toward you.

You may not want to think of yourself as "abused." You might think that happens to other kids, not you. You might want to stay loyal to your parents or friends—after all, if you say you were abused, you are also saying they are abusers. You might feel guilty or ashamed to think of them in this way.

But everyone who has been hurt needs to heal. When your body is hurt, healing organisms go to the place that hurts until, together with prescribed medicine, they heal the injury—usually after some pain. Emotional hurts are the same—they heal with time, and you can often benefit from a helping hand.

This book is that helping hand. The author, Cynthia Mather, speaks knowingly about the confusion, fear, anger, sadness, and despair of incest and sexual abuse. She talks from the point of view of someone who knows, because she herself was hurt when she was young. Her perspective makes sense, and she discusses things in detail, using clear examples. She never suggests that you should figure stuff out on your own. She provides lots of alternatives. She's also very realistic, knowing that some of the suggestions are easier said than done. She wants you to see what your choices are. It's as if she lights up a dark road, so you can see where you are going rather than struggle alone in the dark.

The main thrust of this book is that you can transform this experience from something that scares, confuses, saddens, angers, or makes you feel unsafe or bad about yourself, to something that allows you to feel stronger and prouder about who you are. Cynthia Mather believes (as I do) that you can learn to help yourself by trusting your instincts, giving yourself credit for surviving the experience to begin with, and making choices designed to return the power where it belongs—to you!

July 1994                                                    Eliana Gil, Ph.D.

# Preface

MY NAME IS Cynthia Lynn Mather. I am thirty-nine years old, have been married to the same man for seventeen years, and have two sons aged twelve and nine. I am an amateur musician, a writer, and a lousy cook.

I am also a survivor of incest.

My biological father began sexually abusing me when I was six years old. The physical part ended when I was fourteen, but the verbal sexual abuse continued until I was seventeen.

In the past twenty-some years, I have spent a lot of time, energy, money, and tears trying to deal with the damage my father did to my life. I have finally achieved a place in my own healing where I feel able to reach out to other people who have been sexually abused.

This book started out to be a book for adult women who were trying to heal from the hurt of sexual abuse—until the night a teenage friend blurted out a story about her girlfriend who had been sexually abused by a grandfather. Allison had gone to the library to look for books about incest and sexual abuse so she would know how to help her friend. She couldn't find anything useful.

Suddenly a lightbulb went off in my head: teenagers need a book about sexual abuse and incest—a book that would talk to them about their own unique problems and issues, that would help them through the rough spots and get them started on the road to healing.

My hope is that this book will do just that for you. I have tried to answer many of the questions you may have about sexual abuse. I have also tried to provide basic information, like who are abusers, why do they do it, how can you make them stop, what do you say to your friends, what happens in court, and more.

It's important that as you read this book you remember that every teenager's situation is unique. What happened to one teen may not have happened to you. How you feel about the abuser may be different from what another teen feels. There is no "right" or "wrong" way to feel or be when it comes to sexual abuse. The purpose of this book is to help you see that what you're going through happens to a lot of kids, that however you are feeling is okay, and that there *is* life after sexual abuse.

There have been some very brave teens who allowed me to interview them and others who told me about their abuse through a questionnaire. Many of the comments in this book are either actual quotes from these kids or are combinations of their responses. Some of the comments are from survivors I know personally, have met, or have read about. All comments are based on actual events and conversations but have been changed in some way to protect the privacy of the victims.

My greatest wish is that you'll learn from this book that you are not alone, that you are not bad, that you didn't cause your own abuse, and that it's possible to move on from the pain.

You are a person of great courage, a person to be admired and respected. You may not believe that right now, but I hope you will after you've read this book.

Cynthia L. Mather                                        July 1994
P.O. Box 160
Timonium, MD 21094-0160

# THE HURTING BEGINS

# PART
# ONE

## THE HURTING BEGINS

# 1

## You're Not Alone

It was seven o'clock in the evening. I walked unsuspectingly into my mother's bedroom to ask her a question about my homework. I stopped in my tracks at the doorway. She was dressed in her favorite turquoise dress, had her "going out for the evening" makeup on, and was spraying herself with perfume.

"What are you doing?" I asked in dismay.

"Tonight is my night to play cards with the girls. Remember?" she casually responded.

I had not remembered. The blood drained from my face as I realized that once again, this would be a night of terror. A night of trying to outrun, outsmart, outdistance my father. And once again, my mother was leaving me alone, unprotected and at the mercy of my father.

I WAS TWELVE YEARS OLD that night and believed I was the only person in the world who was living a nightmare. Twenty-seven years later, I know that there are literally thousands of kids who face this scene or something like it every day of their lives, kids who are trying to protect themselves from the very people who are supposed to love them and take care of them. These kids are being sexually abused by people in their lives whom they have a right to trust and believe will not hurt them. These are the kids for whom this book is written.

You may be reading this book as a friend of someone who has been sexually abused. You may be reading it because you're wondering if something that has happened to you is sexual abuse. Or you may be very sure that you have been sexually abused and want some information, some help.

Whatever circumstances have brought you to this book, I'm glad you're reading it. Take your time with it. Sexual abuse and incest are heavy topics. Don't push yourself. This book is designed to help you, not hurt you. Skip around and read the parts that relate to your life right now. Save the other issues for when you are ready to deal with them. If it's best for you, read the book cover to cover. The main thing is to use it for your benefit. If you find you're getting upset or scared, put it away for a while. Let this book work *for* you in your healing, not against you.

## WHAT EXACTLY ARE SEXUAL ABUSE AND INCEST?

First, let's try to get down some definitions of what we'll be talking about. There are many different ways that people define the words *sexual abuse* and *incest*. People in the legal system like judges and lawyers use definitions that talk about "degree" and "temporary care and custody." People in the mental health community (therapists, psychologists, psychiatrists, and others) talk about "betrayal" and "boundary infringement." Other people say, "There is no such thing, so get out of my face."

Well, there *are* such things as sexual abuse and incest and for our purposes in this book, we are going to define *sexual abuse* like this:

Sexual abuse is taking advantage of a child through any act that is designed to sexually stimulate a child or to use a child to sexually stimulate someone else.

This means that if someone in your life is doing one or more of the following things to you, then it's a good bet you are being sexually abused:

1. Penetrating your vagina or anus with fingers, a penis, or other objects

2. Getting you to touch his or her private parts (vagina, breasts, penis, backside)

3. Having you look at sexual pictures or making you pose for sexual pictures

4. Exposing himself or herself to you

5. Finding ways to see you naked or partially undressed

6. Touching you in ways that make you feel uncomfortable

7. Talking to you about sex in ways that make you feel nervous

8. Talking to you about your body or other personal things in ways that make your stomach get tight

This is not a complete listing of what sexual abuse can be. There are hundreds of ways to abuse kids sexually; these are just some examples.

So what about incest? I'm using the term *incest* when the person who is sexually abusing you is a member of your family or someone who has some sort of kinship role in your life.

Incest is sexual abuse of a child by a person who is a member of the child's family or has some type of kinship role in the child's life.

A *member of the family* is someone to whom you are related by blood, like your *biological*

1. Mother or father

2. Brother or sister

3. Aunt or uncle

4. Grandmother or grandfather

5. Cousin

Someone who has a *kinship role* in your life would be someone who is not related to you by blood but has a family type of role in your life. This could be

1. A foster parent

2. A stepparent

3. A guardian

4. An in-law (brother-in-law/sister-in-law)

5. Your mom's live-in boyfriend or dad's live-in girlfriend

6. Anybody who becomes a member of the family through marriage, the law, or circumstances

## A LEGAL DEFINITION

It's important to keep in mind that most state laws define incest as *sexual intercourse between people who are related by blood* (like a brother and sister, a father and daughter, or a grandparent and grandchild). For the purposes of this book, however, we are going to define incest as *any* type of sexual abuse by a family member or someone in a kinship role. This is a pretty wide definition of incest and you may run into some people working in the field of sexual abuse and incest who use a more narrow definition.

Additionally, the legal definition of sexual abuse depends on where the abuse took place, the type of abuse, and whether the abuser had "care and custody" of the child.

So don't let it confuse you if the definitions I'm using here don't match the definitions of lawyers or social workers or the police. The bottom line is that it is abuse and it is against the law.

## ABUSERS OUTSIDE THE FAMILY VERSUS ABUSERS INSIDE THE FAMILY

Let's go even further with our definitions and divide sexual abuse by abuser: abusers who are outside the family and abusers who are members of the family.

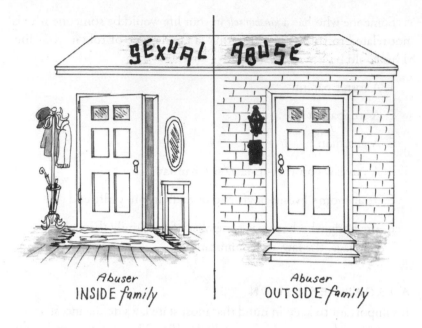

Abuser
INSIDE *family*

Abuser
OUTSIDE *family*

An *abuser who is outside the family* could be

• A teacher

• A coach

• A babysitter

• A religious leader like a priest, minister, or rabbi

• A school janitor

• A doctor

• A scout leader

If any of these people had sexual contact with a child, it would be considered *sexual abuse* because they would have had *care and custody* of the child. This simply means that the child didn't have any choice about being in the situation. He or she was stuck with this person because at that time the adult was in charge of the child.

Lots of kids in this country are sexually abused by people who are not members of their families. In fact, studies show that one out of every three women in this country will be sexually abused by someone *outside* her family by the time she is eighteen.[1] Just ask Heather, who was sexually abused by the father of the children she babysat every Saturday night; or Justine, who was sexually abused by her softball coach; or Gwen, who was sexually abused by her science teacher.

In all these cases, the abuser was someone the victim knew, maybe even someone he or she liked and trusted. The majority of kids are abused by people they see regularly in their lives, people they have a right to believe will not hurt them. Very few kids are sexually abused by strangers. Unfortunately, parents generally tell their kids only to be careful of strangers and never mention that someone they know, or even love, can sexually abuse them.

More commonly, kids are sexually abused by members of their family. An *abuser who is inside the family* or who shares a kinship role with the victim could be a *biological, step, or foster*

- Mom or dad

- Sister or brother

- Grandma or grandpa

- Aunt or uncle

- Cousin

or any *in-laws* (brother-in-law, sister-in-law, and so on). We are calling this type of sexual abuse *incest*.

Incest is set apart from other forms of sexual abuse by the element of family or kinship. As many as one out of every four girls in this country will be sexually abused by someone *in* her family.

Girls like Sharon, who considered her mother's boyfriend a member of the family until he began to fondle her and treat her like a girlfriend; or Yvonne, whose stepfather fondled her from the time she was six and then raped her when she was eleven; or Belinda, who was tortured and sexually abused by her mother and grandmother. All of

---

1. My figures on the scope of child sexual abuse rely on the following sources: *The Best Kept Secret* by Florence Rush, *The Secret Trauma* by Diana E. H. Russell, *Sexually Victimized Children and Child Sexual Abuse* by David Finkelhor, *A Sourcebook on Child Sexual Abuse* by Diana Sullivan Everstine and Louis Everstine, and *By Silence Betrayed* by John Crewdson.

these girls believed that the people who abused them cared about them or loved them. They felt that these abusers were members of the family circle and therefore, safe to trust.

Trust is one of the most important things that sexual abuse destroys. And unfortunately, the closer the abuser is to the abused, the bigger is the break in trust. When someone whom you consider to be "family" sexually abuses you, it can be even harder to pick yourself up and move on.

## ABUSERS WHO FALL INTO THE GRAY AREA

We know that when abuse is committed by people outside the family who have charge of the child (*care and custody*), it's called *sexual abuse*; when it's perpetrated by people inside the family it's called *incest*. But what about those people who fall into the gray area between inside the family and outside the family? Or people who aren't really responsible for the child's care or custody?

Let's take care and custody first. If the person who is abusing you does not have care and custody of you—does not have charge of you for periods of time like a teacher or a coach or a scout leader or a parent or a relative—then the law in many states would call this type of sexual contact *sexual assault* rather than *sexual abuse*. This differentiation is important in terms of how the courts would handle this crime. Yes, sexual assault, just like sexual abuse and incest, is a crime. This differentiation doesn't mean a thing when we talk about the damage this abuse may have caused to your life.

Then there is the abuser who isn't a bona fide member of the family but lives in the same house with the victim. This is what happened in Darnella's case. Her brother's best friend moved in with the family because his own family was so abusive. After two months of living with Darnella's family, he began to find ways to brush against her, fondle her, and eventually rape her. Darnella had a right to believe that this boy would not hurt her. She was not being stupid when she looked at him as another "brother." He was invited to become a part of her family and she viewed him that way. The fault is with her brother's friend, the abuser.

In some states, this abuse would be considered *sexual assault* because this boy did not have care and custody of Darnella. In other states, this abuse would be considered *sexual abuse* because the boy was a member of Darnella's household.

Don't let the language throw you. No matter who does it, what your state's laws call it, or how often it happens; it still hurts, it's still a crime, and it still needs to be dealt with.

## WHAT ABOUT GUYS?

We know now that one out of every three girls in this country will be sexually abused by someone outside her family and that one out of every four girls in this country will be sexually abused by someone inside her family. But what about guys?

It's difficult to get statistics on sexual abuse of boys because guys have a lot of trouble dealing with the idea that they are victims. In our society, men are never supposed to be weak or vulnerable, so if a boy is sexually abused, he may very well block it from his memory or decide that it wasn't really sexual abuse after all. Additionally, many guys start thinking that they are homosexual if they are abused by a male.

William believed that. He thought his parish priest had specifically picked him out from the other boys because somehow he could tell that William was gay. Ridiculous! Guys are not homosexuals because they are abused by a man, just like girls are not lesbians if they are abused by a female.

The best statistics to date say that one out of every seven, maybe as many as one out of every five, boys in this country will be sexually abused by *somebody* by the time they are eighteen.

### YOU'RE NOT ALONE

While these statistics can overwhelm you, they may also make you feel a little better: you are not alone. Thousands of kids in this country are either being sexually abused or are trying to heal from the effects of sexual abuse.

The purpose of this book is to help you become a part of the group that is healing. Believe it or not, it's possible. But first you have to accept the fact that you were a victim.

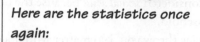

Here are the statistics once again:

*One out of every three girls in this country will be sexually abused by someone outside her family by the time she reaches the age of 18.*

*One out of every four girls in this country will be sexually abused by someone inside her family by the time she reaches the age of 18.*

*One out of every seven, maybe as many as one out of every five, boys in this country will be sexually abused by someone by the time he reaches the age of 18.*

## BELIEVING THAT YOU WERE A VICTIM

The current term for people who have been sexually abused is *survivor*. Some folks say that if you were sexually abused and are still standing, then you are a survivor. I sort of agree with that.

But being a survivor is the *goal;* you have to be a victim of something before you can be a survivor. And that's exactly what you were—a victim—and you were the victim of a crime.

## SEXUAL ABUSE IS A CRIME

Sexual abuse is a crime in every state in this country. Whether the crime is considered a *felony* (resulting in severe punishments) or a *misdemeanor* (resulting in less severe punishments) can be different from state to state. This variation occurs because each state is allowed to decide what circumstances make the abuse a felony or a misdemeanor. The bottom line is still that all sexual abuse is some sort of crime in all states.

## THE ABUSE WAS NOT YOUR FAULT

I'm going to tell you this over and over again, so make sure you get it: the abuse was not your fault!

I know it may be a very difficult concept for you to accept. You may have been told by the abuser that the abuse is all your fault, that he wouldn't be like this if it weren't for you. Junk! Garbage!

The abuse is never, ever the fault of the victim. Understanding this will be your first step to becoming a survivor. If you don't believe it right now, don't worry; you'll hear a lot more about this later on.

For now, let's see what we've learned:

1. Sexual abuse is the big label and incest refers to sexual abuse committed by a family member or someone in a kinship role.

2. Abuse is never the victim's fault; the responsibility is always the abuser's.

3. Sexual abuse *does* happen; it's not something kids make up or lie about; it's a real problem in our society.

4. You're not alone; sexual abuse is happening to a lot of kids out there.

Now let's talk about what may be happening in your life.

# 2

# Is What Happened Really Abuse?

*Every time I went to a slumber party or spent time with one of my friends, I just wanted to ask, "Does your father do these things to you?" I really wanted to know if what was happening was normal or not.*

KARLA, FIFTEEN-YEAR-OLD ABUSED BY STEPFATHER

LIKE KARLA, you may be wondering whether some things that are being done to you are normal or not. It can really be hard sometimes to decide whether abuse is happening or if the touch on your breast was just an accident, the comment about the size of your penis was just rudeness, or if the "funny look" on your uncle's face was just your imagination.

There's another thing that makes it hard to decide whether it's abuse or not: much sexual abuse happens under the disguise of love and attention. Bath time is often the setting for sexual abuse. So is bedtime.

Abusers frequently use these opportunities to fondle and/or sexually stimulate kids. Abusers also use other moments of physical contact to abuse kids: wrestling on the floor, sitting on the couch to watch TV, tickling, driving in the car, "games" that involve touching the child.

There are hundreds of opportunities in a day to have physical contact with a child and therefore, hundreds of chances to abuse that child.

This also means that there are hundreds of opportunities for kids to think that there's something wrong with them.

## I THINK I MIGHT BE CRAZY

How many times have you thought that you were going nuts? I mean totally crazy, off the deep end, ready for the loony bin? I bet it's been lots of times. Cheer up, you're not alone. Most kids who have been sexually abused spend a lot of time believing that they are nuts, psycho, and ready to be put away.

Here's the reason: sexual abuse is such an unexpected thing in a child's world that you have difficulty believing it happened. It's very reasonable to ask yourself, "Why would big sister (or Dad or Mom or babysitter or coach or next-door neighbor) do this to me?"

It's especially confusing if that person says nice things to you or does nice things to you. For example, the coach of your soccer team always tells you what a great job you're doing out there on the field; he couldn't get along without you; if he had his way, you'd be voted most valuable player. Nice stuff, right?

Then, while he's driving you home, he starts saying things like how during showers he noticed you were really developing into a man. He begins commenting on the size of your penis and how some day you're going to make some girl real happy. All of a sudden, the good feeling is gone and now you're feeling embarrassed, confused, maybe frightened. And you don't know what to do.

On the one hand you like the attention and the good stuff he says about you. On the other hand you hate the noise about your body and the personal comments.

Or, let's say you're being abused by your brother. Here you are living in this "family" with all these people who may think your brother is great. He's captain of the football team, makes great grades, works hard at an after-school job, and as far as your parents are concerned, he can do no wrong. And yet, every time you're alone with him, you live in fear of what he's going to do to you. Because of his bigger size, he can overpower you, fondle you, make you perform oral sex on him, or even rape you.

There you are with this picture of who your brother is in the family and the community. You also have a picture of who your brother is when he's abusing you. So you start wondering what's wrong with you instead of wondering what's wrong with him.

Nothing is wrong with you. You are not nuts.

## SEXUAL ABUSE IS CONFUSING

It is definitely okay to see these contradictions in your life, to see that a person can make you feel good sometimes and make you feel really bad other times. It's all right to look at the picture of the abuser as your family or the community sees him or her and realize that this isn't the picture you have.

What's not okay is for you to beat yourself up about it. You are seeing the truth. Did you get that? *You are seeing the truth.* What makes you feel like you're going nuts is that *you are the only one* who is seeing it. And that can get very lonely and very scary.

I can't think of anything on this earth as confusing as sexual abuse. There is no way you can maintain a steady course through your life when you are being bounced around by sexual abuse. You are not nuts, crazy, psycho, or ready to be put away. You are simply seeing what is real. Trust yourself.

## IT'S OKAY TO TRUST YOURSELF

At some point during the abuse, most kids begin to feel uncomfortable, nervous, confused, or scared. They may not look at the abuse in terms of right or wrong, but instead they start to wonder if all kids have this sort of situation in their lives. They tell themselves that the abuser is considered an upstanding adult or is thought of highly by other people, so how could he be doing something wrong?

They start to doubt themselves and their perceptions of what's happening. They begin to buy into the idea that they are nuts or crazy and the abuser is the sane one. They start taking seriously comments the abuser may be making like, "You seduced me"; "You're so pretty, I can't help myself"; or "You wanted it."

Nonsense! Nobody wants to be abused. Yes, people do want love and attention and will often pay extremely high prices for that love and attention, but nobody "wants" abuse.

## HOW DID I LET THIS HAPPEN?

The abuser can also show you "normal" affection and love. He or she can interact with you in a nonsexual way. In fact, you may end up having a good "ordinary" time with the abuser. When this happens, you may really start to think you're crazy. You start telling yourself, "Maybe I just imagined those things. Obviously, this person loves me."

Or you may become hopeful and believe that the abuse is over, a thing of the past. You may look for ways to spend time with the abuser because you really want to have a trusting, loving relationship with him. Then when you get re-abused, you start to wonder, "How did I let this happen?"

*You* didn't let this happen. *You* didn't have anything to do with it. It's human nature to want to trust people, to believe that they won't hurt you. The person who "let it happen" is the abuser.

## THE ABUSE IS NOT YOUR FAULT

We've already talked about this, but I'm going to keep reminding you that the abuse was not your fault. However, if you're having trouble believing that, you're not alone. One of the most common beliefs among sexual abuse victims is that the abuse was their fault, their responsibility. It's often much easier to believe that you are at fault than to believe that someone you want to respect or love or admire is doing something wrong.

Well, here's the news:

Extra! **The Times** Extra!

*YOU WERE NOT RESPONSIBLE FOR THE ABUSE*

That is the fact, and any therapist, psychiatrist, or person with half a brain will back this up. There are people out there who will try to convince you that this was your fault. They are wrong. The abuse is not your fault.

# I DON'T WANT TO BELIEVE IT WAS ABUSE

Kids will go to great lengths to convince themselves that what is happening is not a bad thing. They don't do this because they're stupid. They do it because, like every other kid on the face of the earth, they want to believe that their world is safe and the people in their world are loving and trustworthy. But when kids start experiencing things that make a lie out of that thinking, they may spend a lot of time trying to put a different spin on it. The next sections talk about some of the ways kids try to tell themselves abuse isn't really happening.

## THIS MUST BE LOVE

Abusers do not often start out in a violent way. They usually begin very slowly with a touch here or a suggestive comment there. They try very hard not to frighten the child and often wrap the abuse up in a package of "love and attention." Most kids will respond to loving attention. That's how kids are made. They like to have people spend time with them, offer them special treats, and make them feel loved.

It can become very difficult to decide whether what's happening is okay or not. Sometimes kids enjoy the physical closeness and physical feelings that can happen in an abuse situation. They seek out the abuser for the attention they know they will get and the good feelings they will have.

> It felt good to me and I wanted it.
> ZOE, FIFTEEN-YEAR-OLD ABUSED BY OLDER BROTHER

> It was my mom's boyfriend and he treated me like his girl-friend—holding my hand when we went through the mall, telling me I was so good-looking. I felt special.
> SUZANNE, FOURTEEN-YEAR-OLD ABUSED BY MOTHER'S BOYFRIEND

I liked it in a way. I kind of felt loved. He'd always be there
for me.

KATHERINE, SIXTEEN-YEAR-OLD ABUSED BY BIOLOGICAL FATHER

It's very difficult to figure out whether this is "normal" love and
affection. If you've been abused from a very early age, you may have
nothing to compare it to and may have no clue what "normal" love
looks like between an adult and a child.

## HE DIDN'T MEAN IT—IT MUST HAVE BEEN AN ACCIDENT

Other kids think they are overreacting to an episode of abuse. They
think that what happened was just an accident. They say to themselves, "Oh, she didn't mean to touch me there," or "I guess this is how
all fathers (or grandfathers or uncles or mothers or babysitters or
coaches) act with kids." When the cuddling and attention begins to
make their stomachs tighten and their radar go on full alert, they start
to wonder what's wrong with them. Surely, grandma (or brother or
sister or aunt or family friend) would not hurt them or frighten them.
So the victim begins to think he's weird because he's having a bad reaction to what the abuser is doing.

One night, I fell asleep on the family room sofa while I was
watching TV. I was kind of awake and kind of asleep. I heard
my stepfather come into the room. He came over to the
sofa and leaned over to cover me with the afghan. I didn't
think too much about it until I felt his hand brush against
my breast. I froze. I didn't know what to do: open my eyes,
pretend I was sleeping, jump up and run out of the room,
scream. I just didn't know. I told myself I was being silly
and it was only an accident. Except that over the next
several months, he found lots of opportunities to brush
against my breasts, or my butt, or my legs. I kept telling
myself he wasn't doing it on purpose; maybe I was being
clumsy or all this was my imagination. I told myself a lot of
things until finally I couldn't do it anymore. Then I told my
mother.

ANITA, SEVENTEEN-YEAR-OLD ABUSED BY STEPFATHER

Reason #185
Why I don't want
to believe it was abuse...

## I DESERVE THIS

Still other kids believe that whatever is happening to them is something they deserve. They may feel like they are such scum or slime that they shouldn't be treated nicely or with respect. Or they may believe that they have done something dreadfully wrong and this is their punishment.

> I grew up in a "Christian" home. I believed in a God who "got you" when you were bad. I figured this was God's way of punishing me. The trouble is I couldn't figure out what I had done that was so horrible.
> MARTY, SIXTEEN-YEAR-OLD ABUSED BY HIS STEPFATHER

## ADULTS NEVER DO WRONG

Sometimes kids have simply had "adults are always right" or "you are always wrong" drummed into their heads so much that they can't even begin to think that the abuser could do something bad or unjust. They may be caught by religious teachings to honor their parents or simply have been told that Mom and Dad are always right—no matter what.

> I remember one night when my father snuck into my room. He started his usual stuff, you know, the groping and touching and that stupid laugh. I don't know, something just snapped in me and I jumped off the bed. I ran down the stairs to the front door. He hollered down to me, "Meghan, get back here."
>
> I stood at the front door thinking, who would believe me? Who would take me in? Who would protect me? And then the words, "Thou shalt honor thy father and thy mother," went floating through my head and I went back up those stairs. There was nothing else for me to do.
>
> MEGHAN, FOURTEEN-YEAR-OLD ABUSED BY BIOLOGICAL FATHER

## BUT SHE NEVER TOUCHED ME

Another form that sexual abuse can take is noncontact abuse. Instead of touching the child, the abuser might just talk to the child: make sexual comments about the child's developing body or way of walking or dressing, or constantly put a sexual overtone on conversations. Or the abuser might do things that make the child uncomfortable, like walking in when the child is getting dressed or taking a bath; walking around naked or in underwear in front of the child; using the bathroom with the door open, knowing the child can see. Other forms of noncontact abuse can be showing pornography to a child or taking pornographic pictures of a child.

Sometimes, noncontact abuse is extremely subtle and doesn't look like abuse. Kids who have been sexually abused in this manner often talk about an "atmosphere" in the house where *everything* has a sexual overtone or implication.

> My father took all the doors off the bedrooms and the bathrooms. Nobody had any privacy. You couldn't go to the bathroom, get a shower, get undressed, sleep—nothing— in private. Oh, God, and then when my parents had sex — it was awful.
>
> RICHIE, FIFTEEN-YEAR-OLD ABUSED BY HIS BIOLOGICAL FATHER

Please understand that family members who walk around naked or half-dressed or who accidentally come into the bathroom while you are in there are not necessarily abusers. Some families are very casual about the amount of clothing they wear in their homes. All families have their own rules. What is considered normal and okay in one household may not be in another. The measuring stick is *you* and *your* reaction to these incidents. If you are uncomfortable or these things make you get that "uh-oh," stomach-tightening feeling, then this could be abuse.

The best way to decide what is really happening is to ask the person who is making you uncomfortable to stop doing these things. If he or she dismisses your feelings, tells you you're too sensitive, or seems to be getting pleasure from your discomfort, then that person is being abusive and you need to get someone (an adult you trust) to intervene for you. Noncontact abuse is very subtle but just as damaging as other forms of abuse.

## BUT HE LOOKS SO NORMAL

Another reason you may not be sure whether you've been abused is that the abuser is someone who is known to you and possibly someone you love. All of a sudden you have to rethink what you know about this person. You may end up not being able to believe that this "normal" person could do such abnormal things.

It's difficult to believe that a person who holds down a job, who may be well known, has friends and is well liked, or may be active in the community or church is a child molester. It's much easier to believe that *you* are nuts—especially when you see the abuser acting like a loving, concerned, mature, responsible person. You may get up the morning after an episode of abuse and walk into the kitchen to find the abuser eating Cheerios and reading the morning paper. He's full of smiles and kisses your mother good-bye on his way to work. Instead of asking, "What's wrong with this picture?" you may be asking "What's wrong with me?"

It is also very hard to comprehend that somebody who's supposed to love you is doing these things. It's much easier to believe that you imagined it, that you did something to "deserve" this treatment, or that this happens to all kids.

# I KNOW I WAS ABUSED,
# BUT . . .

If you were raped, you are probably pretty clear that what happened to you was sexual abuse. You were probably also terrified. Not only was the rape unexpected but it may have hurt a lot.

Rape is one of the most violent forms of sexual abuse. A child's vagina or anus is not built to handle an adult penis or other large objects. Therefore, many kids who are raped are also injured with bleeding and pain. If you have been physically injured because of the abuse, seek medical treatment. Go to your school nurse; if you are able to drive, take yourself to your doctor; go to your local emergency room; call an ambulance if necessary. Do not even consider risking your health and your future because you are afraid that the abuse will be uncovered. You are too important to risk!

## BUT HE CAN'T HELP IT

While you may be clear that rape is a hurtful and abusive event, you may feel that you have to put up with it because the abuser can't help himself. Maybe he is an alcoholic or has a drug problem. Maybe you've bought into the idea that you are causing the abuse and the abuser has no choice but to give in to your "charms." There are dozens of ways you may have convinced yourself that this is simply your lot in life, that you have to be the outlet for the abuser's unhappiness.

## BUT I DON'T KNOW HOW I FEEL

Kids tend to have a lot of different kinds of emotions about the abuse and the abuser. Sometimes they feel conflicting emotions like love and hate at the same time; sometimes they want the abuser to die, and then they feel guilty because "you're not supposed to wish anybody dead." Keep in mind that there is no "correct" way to feel about the abuse. You probably have a hodgepodge of feelings and it will take some time for you to sort them out.

## BUT SHE TELLS ME IT'S NOT ABUSE

Abusers are very creative in their efforts to absolve themselves of blame. Besides telling the victim that he or she is responsible for the abuse, abusers will often try to convince themselves as well as the victim that what is happening is normal, loving, appropriate.

Trust your feelings, your perceptions, your view of what's happening. If you are feeling uneasy, self-conscious, nervous, scared because of what someone is doing to you, it's probably abuse. If the things that happen make you uncomfortable, if your stomach clenches and your radar goes on alert, then you are not imagining things. Don't let anybody talk you out of what you know to be true. If you think you are being abused, then it's quite possible you are.

## CAUTION: ABUSE CAN BUILD OVER TIME

If you haven't been raped at this point, don't fool yourself into believing that you're not in danger of being raped. Frequently, other forms of abuse like fondling, masturbating a child, oral sex, or showing pornography are all a build-up to rape. It's been proven that the longer the abuse continues, the worse the abuse can become.

Yes, I am trying to scare you. Yes, I am trying to get you thinking. Yes, I am being dramatic—because, I don't want any more abuse to happen to you. I want you to get out of the abusive situation.

Remember:

- Abuse is against the law.

- Abuse is wrong.

- Abuse always hurts someone.

I want you to get safe and I want you to do it now.

## BUT THERE'S NOTHING I CAN DO

Up to this point you may have believed that there is nothing you can do to protect yourself, that you have zero power and you are simply at the mercy of the abuser. These are very normal responses to the terrifying and hurtful things you are experiencing.

You *do* have some power and some control, however. You *can* protect yourself, and you have many options for getting safe. *But*, and this is the big but, you have to tell. The only way to get safe, the only way to find your power, is by giving up the secret, and giving up the secret means telling.

Come on. You can survive telling. Turn the next page and find out how you're going to get safe.

# BLOWING THE WHISTLE

# 3

## Telling

"Tell? No way. Nobody would believe me."

"You must be on drugs. I would never tell. This would kill my mother."

"Not a chance! They'd put me in some foster home or something."

"Huh-uh. Then we'd have to go to court and everybody would know about it."

OH, I CAN HEAR YOU RIGHT NOW. And you probably know all the other 368 reasons kids give as to why they won't tell. Maybe you're afraid the abuser will hurt you or someone you love. Maybe you're afraid the abuser will be sent to jail or your friends will turn their backs on you. Maybe you think your family will become poor or they will never again be able to hold their heads up. Or maybe you have one of the biggest fears of all: no one will believe you.

Well, the truth is that any or all of these things could happen. I know this sounds bizarre, but that's still no reason not to tell.

You see, if you don't tell, if you don't get someone to intervene on your behalf, then it's very possible that the abuse is going to continue. It's also possible that other kids will be abused, too. But there are things you can do to get the abuse to stop and to get yourself safe.

## HOW TO GET SAFE

There are three steps to getting safe:

You can't get safe as long as the abuse is continuing. And the abuse may continue until you get someone to help you stop it. And that means telling someone that you are being abused.

I know. This is the one thing you have spent your life avoiding—telling anyone what is *really* happening in your life. But the time has come to give up the secret. You are valuable and important and you deserve to have a life free of abuse. So let's get safe.

## THE FIRST STEP—TELLING

You have lots of options for finding someone to help you.

### Your Mother

Many kids think that this kind of news would kill their mother. They think their mom will just curl up and die if they reveal what's been happening. It's true that what you have to tell your mother will hurt her. She may even call you a liar or worse. I'm not trying to excuse a mother's disbelief; I'm just saying that sometimes it's easier to yell, "Liar!" than to face the enormity of the truth.

However, you need to let your mother make the choice of how she is going to react to your telling. Mothers are not as fragile as you think. If you can get beyond her initial reaction (which may be horrible), she may turn out to be a big source of support.

Here's how it went for Georgia, a heavy-set girl with beautiful brown eyes. Georgia wants to be a beautician when she grows up, and she does a lot of experimenting with makeup, which makes her look older than fourteen.

I was eleven when my brother tried to rape me while he was babysitting us kids. He was fifteen and should have known better.

About six months after my parents divorced, Gary started getting into bed with me and my sister. There was a bad storm the first time and we were scared, so he was gonna comfort us, you know. But after that he started finding excuses for gettin' into bed with us and then he starts touchin' places he's got no business touchin'.

Well, before you know it, he's trying to get me and my sister to touch his penis and he's pulling on our breasts. I kept telling my mother that Gary was bothering us girls at night. But she didn't want to hear about it. She just blew it off.

Then one night when my mother was out, Gary threw me on the couch and started ripping off my clothes. I was screaming and carryin' on and finally he stopped.

When my mother came home, I told her what happened and she called up the Protective Services. A social worker came to talk to me. She talked to my sister and my mother, too. The police talked to my brother.

It turns out that my mother had actually walked in one time when Gary was in bed with us and had seen what he was doing. She says she figured we had agreed to what was going on. Is this woman for real?

Well, the judge said Gary can't see me and my sister anymore and my mother has to make sure she don't let him come to the house unless our therapist says it's okay. Of course, he ain't goin' anywhere soon cause he got arrested and has to stay in a treatment program where you live and finish your school and get a job. Which is just fine by me.

Georgia's mother at least reported the abuse. Some mothers don't believe their kids at all and won't make a report.

Unfortunately, even though the report was made, Georgia's mother still didn't think too much about the abuse. She continued to "blow it off," to tell her daughters they were making too much of the whole thing. But by reporting the abuse, Georgia's mom did at least get Georgia and her sister safe and free from being abused.

Other mothers come through for their kids in a big way. This is what Mary-Ellen's mom had to say when Mary-Ellen told her what had happened.

I walked in from work and my husband was asleep on the sofa, drunk. Mary-Ellen was crying hysterically. She said, "Dad raped me." I immediately took her to the emergency room. I believed her right away. I wanted to kill that son of a bitch.

These moms believe their children, make reports, get them to a safe place, find a therapist for them, and try to help them move on with their lives. However, it's a rare mother who can do all of this while holding herself and the rest of the family together. But give your mom a chance. She may surprise you with how much she *can* do.

**Your Father**

You may have the same reaction to telling your dad that we talked about under telling mothers—he can't handle it. Well, again, you're never going to know until you give him the chance.

If your father is not the one who is abusing you, he may be a very good resource for getting the abuse stopped. Maybe you don't live with your dad because your parents are divorced. Maybe you don't get to see much of him because he lives far away or because your parents are always fighting about custody and child support. If this is the case, you may not have a very good feel for what his response would be to finding out you are being sexually abused.

However, if there is the slightest chance that he would be in a position to help you, then try telling your dad. Sometimes fathers really come through when they see just how much their child needs them. Think about it. If dad's not the abuser, he may turn out to be your strongest advocate.

**Someone at School**

Many schools nowadays have guidance counselors or social workers who have special training in the mental health fields like psychology or counseling. This person could be a good resource for you.

A favorite teacher is another option. If you have a teacher that you get along with or know of a teacher who is easy to talk to, you might consider telling him or her. Then that person can help you plan how to get the abuse to stop.

Samuel had always liked his English teacher and took advantage of an opportunity that unexpectedly came his way.

> My "Stay Healthy" class had a woman come in and talk to us about sexual abuse. I could barely sit through her talk. It was like she was talking right to me! I could relate to almost everything she said.
>
> I had a really hard time sitting still. I kept tapping my pen and jiggling my foot. I was the first one out of the room when the bell rang. But I couldn't forget it.

This woman had been sexually abused when she was a kid so she knew what she was talking about. The same sentence kept going through my head: "You have to tell. You can't get safe unless you tell."

So I told. I told Miss Marsden, my English teacher. I was really scared. I thought she would hate me after I told her some of the stuff my father did to me. But she was really cool about the whole thing. She told me she had to make a report—that's the law where I live—but she would stay with me during the interviews and would be there for me whenever I needed to talk. And she has.

Many times, teachers or people in the school system *must* make a report because the law says they have to. Don't let that keep you from telling. A report means that the authorities are going to get involved and that means you have a good chance of getting safe.

### A Friend's Parent

When you're in your teens, other kids' parents can seem nicer than your own. Sometimes, it's easier to tell things to the parent of one of your friends than it is to tell your own mom or dad. If that's the case for you, then consider telling the parent or parents of one of your friends. Keep in mind that they will probably be shocked and go through their own struggle of seeing the abuser (if they know him or her) in a different light. However, if they are the kind of people you think they are, they should be able to get their emotions under control and help you get a handle on how to deal with this.

Jamie is fifteen now. She's back home with her parents. But it hasn't been an easy two years getting to this point. She speaks softly and sinks into the chair as she remembers what happened.

I just couldn't take it any more. I had to do something or I would have gone insane. I had told my mother what Albert was doing to me, but she didn't do anything about it. So, I ran away.

It started when I was about five. My parents would go out to a lot of parties and business things. They always had this guy named Albert to babysit me. He drank a lot—maybe that's why he did all this stuff.

Well, he would tuck me into bed and then he would get into bed with me. He would rub my back and ask me to rub his. It all seemed okay at first. But then he would start taking off my clothes and touching my privates. And then when I was about ten, he would . . . oh God this is so embarrassing . . . he would make me put his thing in my mouth. He would hold my head and force me. Or he would hold me down while he put his fingers inside of me or while he sucked on my breasts. . . . God, I hate remembering!

I thought I would be smart and start having friends over when Albert babysat, but he just started doing stuff to them like making comments about their bodies or showing us X-rated movies.

Finally, I told my friend, Michelle, that I was going to either run away or crack up. She told me I could stay at her house. Her parents were really nice to me—didn't ask a lot of questions or press me about anything. After about two weeks, I told Michelle's mother what had been happening. She made the report. She let me stay with them while the investigation was going on. It was the first time in a long time that I felt safe.

Unfortunately, my parents didn't believe me. They got really mad with me and Michelle's parents. I felt terrible. Her parents had been so nice to me and here were my parents saying all this terrible stuff to them.

Well, I had to go into foster care because my parents wouldn't sign some papers or something so that I could stay with Michelle's family. I hated that! Then one of my friends told her parents some of the stuff that had happened when she spent the night at my house, and Albert confessed. Her story made people realize my story was true. And finally, my parents believed me.

I'm still a little bit mad that they didn't believe me right away. But I'm working on it. I'm back home now. Albert's on probation. My parents and I talk a lot more than we used to. The only bad thing is that my parents aren't real friendly with Michelle's parents anymore. I feel kind of guilty about that.

There are adults who will go to bat for you, stand up for you, protect you—even if it costs them a friendship like it did in Jamie's situation. Take a risk. Tell someone.

## A Religious Leader

Many kids attend church, temple, or a youth fellowship. You may find it easier to talk to a Sunday School teacher, minister, rabbi, priest, or youth leader. Don't be put off because the person you choose to tell is religious. There are many abusers sitting in the seats of churches, synagogues, and temples, so the person you select should not try to tell you that someone who goes to church "would never do anything like this." If that's what you are told, move on. Find someone else to tell.

Peter tried telling a youth leader while he was on a retreat with his church group. He was feeling really isolated and different from the other kids. His youth leader, Max, noticed and came over and asked what was wrong.

My heart was pounding and my mouth got really dry. But I don't think I could have kept the words from coming out. All of a sudden I just blurted it out, "My mother touches me in ways that make me uncomfortable."

Max literally drew back away from me and said, "Oh Peter, that's sick."

Well, I right away started denying, "Oh, it's nothing like that!"

And we never talked about it again. I eventually told someone else. But I was really hurt. I mean Max was usually so understanding. He really let me down on this one.

Max did let Peter down. But by telling once, Peter learned he wouldn't be struck by a bolt of lightning; he could tell and still live.

To Peter's credit, he didn't give up. He found someone else to tell who not only believed him, but made a report as well.

Your experience may be totally different from Peter's. Many churches and synagogues today are making strong efforts to educate their congregations as well as their staff about sexual abuse. For example, the Catholic church has recently set up new rules about how to deal with sexual abuse allegations. They haven't had a very good track record of being responsive to the victim or responsible about the abuser. But things are changing for the better.

Don't let Peter's experience stop you from telling someone in your place of worship. If you really believe people there can help, then tell. If it doesn't work out, then, like Peter, move on and find someone else to tell.

You have a lot of choices of who to tell.

### Your Best Friend

If your friend is really your best friend, then she will probably tell an adult about your revelation—whether you want her to or not. A best friend knows that the problem is too big for her to handle alone and that an adult needs to be involved. If your friend tells you that she's going to tell an adult, then at least say which adult you would prefer be told.

A best friend will still be your friend after you tell and will stick by you as the abuse is dealt with. She will tell other people where to go if they start making rude comments about you and the abuse. A best friend can be a real help to you during this time.

Cathy was only ten years old when she told her best friend, Robin, what her stepfather was doing to her. Three years later, she still remembers how angry she was when Robin told the school guidance counselor.

> I remember being called down to Mrs. Dawson's office. I didn't know why she wanted to see me.
>
> When I got to her office, Mrs. Dawson started asking me questions about how things were going at home. After a while, it was obvious she knew about my stepfather. I was so mad! I had told Robin not to tell anyone.
>
> I tried to act like I didn't know what Mrs. Dawson was talking about. But then I started crying. She gave me some tissues and told me this wasn't my fault; my stepfather was wrong to do this stuff to me. Then she said she had to call the police because what Bob had done was against the law.
>
> I was ready to kill Robin. I mean the police! Geez, I was so scared. I kept thinking that if she had kept her mouth shut none of this would be happening.
>
> Now, I'm glad she told.

Cathy was lucky. She and Robin were able to remain friends. Sometimes it's too hard to stay friends with the person who made the report or got an adult involved. In one way, you may be very glad she did because the abuse has been stopped, you've gotten to a safe place, and life is starting to get good. But you don't want to be around your friend because it reminds you too much of what happened.

Another possibility is that things didn't go well after the report was made. Maybe no one believed you, or your family kicked you out, or court was a nightmare. It'd be pretty normal not to want to be around the person who stirred up this mess. Don't spend a lot of time feeling bad about this. Give thanks that the person cared enough about you to step in, and then get yourself moving on with the business of healing.

## A Medical Person

If the abuse has caused you physical problems, especially damage to the vagina or anus, then you have probably been seen by a doctor. If you are asked how these things happened, don't lie. If a parent is in the room with you and you don't want to say in front of him or her, ask the doctor if you can talk privately. Then tell the truth. Doctors and nurses are very aware of sexual abuse. They know the signs and they know how to deal with it. They'll know what to do with the information you give them.

If you are just seeing your doctor for routine stuff, then think about telling him or her. Again, people in the medical professions see sexual and other kinds of abuse all the time. They can help you. If they don't, find someone else to tell.

Angela is eighteen now. But when she turned sixteen and could drive, one of the first places she went was the free clinic. She was afraid that . . . well here, let her tell it.

> I had been having all kinds of, you know, female problems. Stuff coming out of me that had a bad smell, terrible periods, that kind of thing. But when I got these like big pimples all around my bush, I really freaked. I knew I better get a doctor to look at it. So I went to the clinic. Turns out I had herpes and the doctor needed to know who my sexual partners were because my partner had to be treated too so he wouldn't spread it to someone else.
>
> I gotta say, I really got mad. Not only had my uncle treated me like a slut, but he had given me this disease, too. And herpes can really cause me problems—like messed up babies and a bigger chance of getting cervical cancer. So I told the doctor. Once she heard it was my uncle, she called the police and made a report. That was a

hard day. I hated talking to all those people. And now my cousins and my aunt won't speak to me. But my uncle can't touch me any more and the herpes is under control, for now.

Angela learned the hard way about the need to tell; she got a disease from the abuse. In a way, though, Angela was lucky. Herpes won't kill you like AIDS will. If you're still debating whether you should tell, ask yourself if it is worth contracting a sexually transmitted disease that will be with you the rest of your life—or a disease like AIDS that will end your life. Are the abuser or your fears about what will happen after you tell worth dying for? I think not. Tell someone!

## The Police

For some kids, a police officer is the first person they tell because the abuse has reached a crisis point. They fear for their lives or their safety so much that they call 911 without thinking twice about it. That was the situation for Karen. She was thirteen and her brother was sixteen.

My brother had been doing stuff to me for years. You know, things like trying to see me without my clothes on, making comments about my chest when I started to get boobs, exposing himself and saying, "You want some of this, babe?" Just gross stuff like that.

But one weekend my parents went away and left us without a sitter. They figured we were old enough to stay home alone. Well, my brother invited some friends over and they started drinking. They started saying stuff and trying to get me to play strip poker with them. I really wasn't scared at first. I mean, I knew these guys; they came over to our house all the time. But that night they were really different.

I was upstairs doing homework and they were down in the basement. All of a sudden I realized things had gotten really quiet. Then, out of nowhere, my brother pounced on me and hollered, "I got her. Who's going to be first?" I didn't know what he meant right away. And then I saw his buddy, Louis, start unzipping his pants. I absolutely freaked.

I hit my brother as hard as I could and got away from him. Then I ran upstairs to my parents' bedroom because they had a phone. I had to block the door with furniture because I was afraid the lock wouldn't hold. I called the police and told them I was about to be raped. They came within minutes.

For other kids, the police are the last people they would ever consider calling. These kids view the police as the enemy: the person who's going to break up the party, give them a speeding ticket, bust them for drugs. For them, the police are to be avoided.

Brad felt that way, even though his priest had been abusing him for three years, ever since he was eleven and had become an altar boy.

First of all, the police already knew me. We live in a small town and they tend to remember the kids who get into trouble. Second, you just don't turn a priest in to the police. I mean, think about it. Who are they gonna believe? Me, the troublemaker, or the priest, a man of God?

Yeah, call the police. That's a laugh.

You may feel the same way Brad does. But remember, sexual abuse and incest are *crimes*. The degree of the crime may vary from state to state and situation to situation, but they are still against the law. Therefore, the police can be a good place to start.

Most police forces, at least the larger ones, have a special unit that deals only with kids who have been sexually abused. They usually wear regular clothes and drive unmarked cars. When they come to interview you, it's not real obvious that they are the law. Don't be afraid to call the police, especially if the abuse has taken a turn for the worse and you find yourself at a crisis point.

### Special Agencies

There are quite a few agencies and organizations that exist for the purpose of helping people who have been sexually abused. You can make a report to the child protective services agency, which is a part of your local department of social services. To find their number, call information or look in your local government listings in the phone book.

You can call places like The Sexual Abuse and Recovery Center or Sexual Assault and Recovery Center, which can be found in the white business pages or Yellow Pages under Sex. A rape crisis center is another agency that can help people who have been sexually abused.

As they say, let your fingers do the walking, and call someone today.

### Other People

There are probably many people in your life who you feel are capable and trustworthy. You may not have tried trusting them yet, but now could be the time to give it a shot. Perhaps there is a relative (a favorite aunt or grandparent) who you think would listen and believe you. Let these people make the choice of how they are going to handle the news. Don't decide for them. You may miss a perfect opportunity for getting help in stopping the abuse.

> IMPORTANT: If anyone does not believe you, calls you a liar, a whore, a queer, a troublemaker or worse, move on. It's easier said than done. But there are people who will believe you and who will give you the compassion and understanding you deserve.

### THE SECOND STEP—REPORTING

Anyone you tell who says, "Gee, that's too bad," pats you on the head, and sends you on your way is not doing you a favor. If that happens to you, then tell someone else.

The best thing that anyone who learns of the abuse can do is to contact the authorities. Wait, don't go spinning off the planet. Let me explain.

Authorities on the subject of sexual abuse are exactly the people who can help. They know how to make the abuse stop and see that the abuser gets the help he or she needs to stop abusing kids. And they know how to help you and other members of your family sort through what has happened and begin the healing process.

Some states have laws requiring people to report any suspicion of sexual abuse. Other states get very specific and say that anyone in the educational system (teachers, principals, guidance counselors), the medical profession (doctors, nurses), the social service system (social workers), the mental health professions (psychologists, therapists, counselors), or the police department must report any disclosures of abuse. It's quite possible, depending on the state you live in, that anyone you tell may, by law, have to report what you have said.

This is not necessarily a bad thing. It may be the only way to be sure the abuse stops and you get the chance to move on and be the person you can be.

## What Will Happen After the Report Is Made?

Once you have told someone about the abuse, the best thing would be for that person to make a report to the authorities. Then the authorities will want to talk to you.

You may be wondering just exactly who these "authorities" are. They are all the folks who get involved in any report of sexual abuse or incest, such as the person who takes down the report, like a worker from the local child protective services, a social worker, or a police officer; the people who investigate the report by interviewing the victim, the abuser, and others; the social workers who are responsible for protecting the victim; the district attorney who will prosecute the abuser if that seems appropriate; the doctor or nurse who may be asked to examine you; the therapist who may talk to you about what happened. All these people have one goal and that is to try to find out what happened and to make sure that it doesn't happen again. That's the goal but it's not always the reality. It can be a very tough process.

> Once I told my mother what was going on, I figured that was the end of it . . . that it was all over. I was wrong. It was just the beginning of the next phase of the whole mess.
> BRIANNA, FIFTEEN-YEAR-OLD ABUSED BY STEPFATHER

Some states make it easier on the victim by having all the authorities work together as a team. For instance, in some states when a report of sexual abuse or incest is made, both a detective from the police department and a worker from child protective services will interview the victim together. Then, they meet with the district attorney's office and report on the charges that are being made. This way, the victim doesn't have to tell his story ninety-seven times to ninety-seven different people.

But not every state does it this way. In some states, the agency that received the report sends out a representative to talk to the victim. Then the other agencies talk to the victim as they get involved. This means that if the person you've told about the abuse reports it to the police, then someone from the police department will come and talk to you. Later on the same day, or in a couple of days, a representative from the social services or child protection agency will also come talk to you. Then as the district attorney's office gets involved, you'll be interviewed once again. If medical or psychological personnel are called in—yep, you got it—another interview. This method can get old real fast, but it may be the way things are done in your state. Try to keep your cool and be cooperative.

You can make the report yourself.

### THE THIRD STEP—PROTECTING

After you have been interviewed, the authorities will contact your nonabusing guardian. This would be the person who is responsible for you and who did not abuse you. If your mother's boyfriend was the abuser, then the authorities will contact your mother. If the abuser was someone outside of your family, then they'll contact one or both of your parents. If the abuser was your mother and your father's dead, then they'll contact another relative. You get the idea. Whoever is responsible for your well-being and was not involved in the abuse will be called by the authorities.

Let's say your stepfather abused you and your mother was not involved in the abuse. The authorities would then contact your mother and tell her what you have said and ask for her comments and reaction. As we've already discussed, this is most likely going to be a shock for your mom and she may not handle it well at first. She may say you're a liar, that you're doing this to get attention, that her husband would never do this—any or all of the above. If she cannot come to terms with the fact that you were abused and agree to keep you safe from the abuser, then the authorities have no choice but to find a safe place for you to go while everything gets sorted out.

This may mean that you will go to a foster home for a couple of nights or stay with relatives or a friend. Speak up. It's okay to ask what's happening and make suggestions about where you could stay until things calm down.

### Will the Abuser Find Out About the Report?
One of the things that may have kept you from telling about the abuse is that you're afraid of the abuser—that he will hurt you or even kill you. It is necessary that the abuser be interviewed after the report is made and after you and your guardian have been interviewed. Again, every state is different. Some states have a social worker and a detective interview the abuser together; other states conduct separate interviews.

The bottom line is that within a relatively short period of time, the abuser will know that you have accused him or her of abusing you. This may be a very scary time for you. Don't back away from what you know to be true. If you are afraid for your physical safety, tell the social worker, the police, the doctor, anyone. They can help keep you safe.

My father was away on a hunting trip when I told. The social worker and my mother were really afraid that he would be violent when he got back and found out that I had told. So I had to leave and stay with my friend until the police could talk to him.

JOEY, FIFTEEN-YEAR-OLD ABUSED BY STEPFATHER

### Staying Safe

It's important to remember that the whole concern here is to keep you safe, to keep you away from the abuser until the authorities have time to talk to him and make some decisions. If your mother (or the person responsible for keeping you safe) is unwilling or unable to keep the abuser out of the house and protect you, then the authorities *must* protect you.

Try hard to keep your cool. This can be very frightening and scary. Get somebody to be with you. If the person who made the report can't do it, call someone else to be with you to hold your hand or simply to offer moral support.

Many kids are assigned a social worker who will be in charge of their safety and well-being. If you have a social worker or child protective services worker assigned to you, you may find that he or she can be a real help in keeping you informed of what's happening

There are agencies that can help you to be safe.

and where things are heading. She may also be able to get you involved in therapy, even group therapy with kids your age who have also been sexually abused. (More on therapy in Chapter Eight.)

## TAKING CARE
## OF YOURSELF

There are some things you can do to take care of yourself when you are dealing with the authorities.

### GET SOME SUPPORT

If you really trust and like the person you confided in (the person who made the report), then ask him to be with you during these interviews. Sometimes that's not possible; maybe he is unavailable or maybe the interviewers won't allow it. You don't know until you ask—so ask.

### GET THE FULL STORY

If you don't understand what's going on, say so. If you want an update or an idea of what will happen next, ask. Stand up for yourself and do positive, reasonable things that are going to help you get through this. That could be asking polite questions about what's going to happen to you; politely disagreeing with plans that scare you or make you uncomfortable; politely requesting more information.

### STAY IN CONTROL OF YOURSELF

You'll notice I keep suggesting you be "polite" when in reality you may be ready to spit nails or scream. I encourage you to keep yourself as under control as possible. If you come across as a hysterical, out-of-control adolescent, you're not going to have much opportunity to be a part of the decision-making process about what's going to happen to keep you safe.

### BE HONEST ABOUT YOUR FEELINGS

If you're really struggling to keep it together, say so. It's totally reasonable to say, "I'm very upset right now and want to cry (put my fist through a wall, yell, scream, break something). I'm trying really hard to stay in control so I can be a reasonable part of these decisions." Not only have you stated exactly where you are, but you have also demonstrated that you can manage your feelings and continue functioning in a rational, mature manner. The people you are dealing with may take another look at you and realize that you may have some valuable input to what's going to happen.

## YOU DID GOOD

Blowing the whistle may be one of the hardest things you will ever do in your life. You may start wishing you had kept your mouth shut because things are such a mess. Once the abuser is interviewed and knows that you have made a complaint against him, things may get ugly. The abuser may threaten you or members of his family may threaten you. People may be really rude or mean to you. I'm not going to kid you; getting safe is hard work. But you can do it.

Always remember: you did the right thing by telling. You made a decision for you. You stood up and said, "I matter. I'm important. And I'm not going to put up with this anymore."

You did good. Keep telling yourself that.

# 4

## What Will People Say?

*I was afraid to go to practice. I figured all the guys would make fun of me and call me a faggot or something. Or that they'd be mad at me because I got the coach in trouble. I hated for everyone to know about it.*
HARRY, A SIXTEEN-YEAR-OLD ABUSED BY HIS FOOTBALL COACH

O NE OF THE TOUGHEST THINGS to deal with after you tell about the abuse may be the reaction of other people. Some folks are going to be wonderful. They are going to support you, encourage you, defend you.

A lot of people are going to be awful. Some of it will be because they are just plain stupid. They haven't got a clue about how to deal with someone who has revealed they've been sexually abused.

Some of it will be because they can't deal with the idea of sexual abuse. Maybe they've never been exposed to tough things in their lives; they've had a fairy-tale existence with nothing bad in it. Or maybe your experience hits too close to home and reminds them of abuse they have suffered.

Other people will say ridiculous things like "Why didn't you just tell him to stop?" or "Are you sure you didn't misunderstand what happened?" or, my personal favorite, "I think you should just forget

about it and get on with your life." (Oh, right. Forget my entire childhood and pretend that nothing ever happened. No problem!)

Regardless of what people are saying, the one voice you need to hear
above the others is your own voice reminding you that you did
the right thing by telling. It's not easy to discount or ignore the other
voices. Maybe it will help if we talk about some of the things you can
expect people to say to you.

## WHEN PEOPLE SAY
## YOU'RE LYING . . .

People may be saying this over and over to you. Everybody from your
grandmother to your little sister. The police or social service workers
may be asking you to repeat parts of your story again and again. They
say they want to be sure they have it straight, but you think they don't
believe you.

The parent who did not abuse you (let's say it's your mother) may
be the most vocal about calling you a liar. It can be very hard for a
mother to believe that her husband or boyfriend would do something
like this. It's even harder for a mother to think that she had no idea this
was going on. Your mother has a lot to lose if what you say is true and
she may be constantly in your face claiming you're a liar.

If the abuser is someone outside your family, then you may be taking a lot of heat from his relatives and friends. They may be calling
you a liar and trying to say that the abuse (if they'll even admit it happened) was your fault.

Hang tough. Kids lie to get *out* of trouble; they don't lie to get *into*
trouble. You know what happened. Don't let the accusations make you
give up.

## WHEN PEOPLE SAY
## YOU LED HIM ON . . .

This may be one of the hardest statements to ignore. As we said
before, it's very easy to believe that somehow you were responsible for
your own abuse—that you caused it, led the abuser on, asked for it,
wanted it, and all that other garbage.

The thing to remember is that this kind of talk is garbage. Who is responsible for the abuse? Right, the abuser. I don't care how many times you found yourself in a situation where you might end up being abused, the ultimate responsibility for the abuse is with the abuser. I'm not interested in the way you dressed, talked, acted. It was not your job to control the abuser and his or her actions. The bottom line is that the abuser is responsible— always.

You *do* have a responsibility to learn from some of this stuff and we'll talk about that when we get to healing. But right now, this very minute, you must remember that you were not responsible for the abuse. Go back to page 19 and re-read about people who try to put the blame on you. Do you have any people in your life who are working with less than half a brain? Ignore them.

## WHEN PEOPLE GOSSIP ABOUT YOU...

Some of the toughest encounters you may have are with your friends and schoolmates. School is often the place where the police and social services workers interview a victim of sexual abuse. They see it as neutral ground—away from the abuser and the person who might have protected you.

You, on the other hand, may see it as the worst place in the world. You get called out of class to the principal's office. The secretary knows the police and the social worker are waiting to talk to you. The principal knows and may even stay during the interview, and later all your friends want to know what's going on.

What you tell your friends is up to you. It's nobody's business except yours and the people you want to tell. Yes, some information will leak out. Yes, some people that you didn't tell may know about what happened. And yes, you can survive this. Simply ignore them. Hold your head up. You have nothing to be ashamed of.

You may be tempted to drop out of clubs or other school activities because you think "everybody knows." Don't do it. You need as much stability and continuity in your life as you can get right now. And doing the things you usually do will help you. Being with friends can also help—unless, of course, those "friends" turn out not to be such good friends.

> REMEMBER: You were not responsible for the abuse. There is nothing wrong with you. You are valuable and have a right to be treated like a valuable human being—especially by your friends. Keep your head up.

If anybody snubs you, talks about you behind your back, or spreads rumors and gossip—then she wasn't really a friend in the first place. You will find out who your friends are through all this and will know who to spend time with and who to ignore.

## WHEN PEOPLE SAY YOU'RE DESTROYING THE FAMILY . . .

When sexual abuse or incest invades a family, a lot of anger, fear, and stress occur, not only to the parents of the victim but also to the brothers and sisters, the grandmas and grandpas, aunts and uncles and cousins. Whoever finds out about the abuse is going to have an opinion, and it won't always be an opinion in your favor.

If the abuser is someone in your family (let's say it's your father), then your mom may be saying things like, "Just tell the police you made a mistake and I'll make sure he never touches you again. Otherwise, they're going to put him in jail and he won't be able to work, and we won't have any money, and we'll lose the house and end up on the streets."

Your sister may be begging you to say you were lying because "What will all our friends think when they hear about this?" or "Why do you always have to cause trouble?"

And your grandparents may be trying to save your soul because it's clear to them you're possessed by the devil. After all, their son "would never do this sort of thing."

This stinks! You weren't the one who caused the problem and yet all of a sudden everyone in the family is pointing a finger at you and accusing *you*. Maybe even calling you names like troublemaker, liar, whore.

Unfortunately, this is often how family members deal with revelations of abuse. They have trouble believing it happened and they have trouble controlling their emotions.

## TAKING CARE OF YOURSELF

You may start to feel really beaten down and get on your own case because of all the stress and tension happening in your family. You may start to wonder if the abuse really did happen, if it's really worth it to tell, or if you're maybe losing your grasp of reality. Don't let these doubts eat away at what you know to be true.

It's not easy to stand up to pressure and angry words from the people who are supposed to love you best—your family. But if the abuse happened and you finally worked up the courage to tell about it, don't give up now. As hard as it is, hang in there. Eventually things will simmer down and people will get over their initial shock. You may even find some members of your family becoming very supportive of you and sticking by you through everything.

### What if Nobody Will Stick by You?

If no one will come to your defense, then you're going to have to get a support group on your own. This could be good friends, members of a victims' group you're attending, a therapist or social worker, or an adult in your life such as a teacher or coach. Don't be afraid to ask for support. It's okay to say, "I need somebody to believe me and to stand by me in the face of my family's rejection."

### What if You Have to Move Out for a While?

You may find that you simply can't face your family's anger and accusations. It may be in your best interest to live elsewhere for a while. You can talk to your social worker or therapist about this and see if it's a good idea in your situation.

Deciding to leave won't be easy, but remember that the first priority is you and your well-being. If the people around you won't take care of you or see that you are safe—not just from the abuser but also from the pain of accusations from others—then you may need to stand up and take care of yourself. Your well-being is the number one priority.

## YOUR FAMILY IS RESPONSIBLE FOR THEIR FEELINGS AND ACTIONS

There is no question that the revelation of sexual abuse is tough on a family, but that is not a reason to change your story or say you made this all up. You are not responsible for the abuse and you are not responsible for how your family is feeling and acting. It is grandma's choice, mom's choice, sister's choice, how they want to feel and what they want to do. You are not responsible for them.

However, you do have to live with them or at the very least interact with them. It's going to be important that you have some help learning how to do that. Your social worker can get you and sometimes other family members into some kind of therapy. If no therapy has been offered, speak up and ask for it. Remember, take care of yourself.

## WHEN YOU START BELIEVING WHAT PEOPLE SAY

You may get very good at ignoring what other people are saying. However, there may be one person who is really working on you, trying to convince you that you are responsible for the abuse and that there is something seriously wrong with you. That person may be *you*.

Kids, by nature, view crisis and trouble in their families as somehow their fault. When parents fight, siblings get into trouble, money gets tight, or the breadwinner loses her job, children often believe they did something to make all this happen. So when something as traumatic as sexual abuse happens to a kid, he or she may instantly say, "I'm responsible—I did this." Add to that the subtle and not so subtle messages you're getting from the abuser like, "You're so cute I can't keep my hands off you," or, "You enjoyed it." What are you going to believe? You're going to start believing that you are the cause of your own abuse.

The fact is (everybody all together now) *the child is never responsible for the abuse.* You are the child in the relationship. Even if you are seventeen years old and the abuser is only a couple of years older—or younger!—you're still not responsible. You were used, done to. You were not responsible.

## I SHOULD HAVE STOPPED IT

You may feel that you should have stopped the abuse, that you should have been able to stand up to the abuser and tell him or her to knock it off.

Get a grip. Think about it! How could you have done that? How could you, a kid—maybe three, maybe nine, maybe seventeen—have had any control over the actions of this person who had some sort of power or authority over you or who was bigger or stronger than you? How could you, a smaller, weaker, no-authority kid make the abuser listen to you? There is no way that you could have stopped the abuser by yourself. Absolutely none.

## I SHOULD HAVE BEEN SMARTER

It may be that the abuser told you that he would hurt you if you told anyone about the abuse, or maybe she threatened to hurt someone or something you love. Nobody in his right mind is going to test this threat to see whether it's a bluff—if the abuser was just kidding. If someone threatened you with bodily harm or threatened someone you love, you have some very good reasons for not stopping the abuse. You probably figured that your suffering was keeping others safe. That's logical. Don't get upset with yourself if that's what you believed.

It could be that the abuser simply told you that no one would believe you, or maybe he convinced you that the abuse was all your fault. These statements can be just as paralyzing as the threat of someone's hurting you. If you are told something over and over again—"You'll go to jail if anyone finds out," "No one will listen to you," "You wanted it so it's your fault"—you begin to believe it. This doesn't mean you're stupid or haven't any common sense; it means that you were being abused.

On the other hand, it's possible that you were made powerless by caring too much for the abuser. You may have wanted so much to be loved by the abuser that you disregarded your own feelings. Or you may have worried about the abuser's getting hurt more than about your getting hurt.

If that's your situation, you may have a harder time seeing what's happening as abuse because it's so wrapped up in love and special attention. The abuser may have told you over and over again how special you are, how important to his life you are, how no one else in the world satisfies him the way you do. This is pretty powerful stuff and can be really difficult to disbelieve.

If this is what's happening to you, let's do a reality check. Being special *is* important, but it doesn't mean you have to ignore your own feelings and needs. Being special can help us feel good about ourselves, but it doesn't have to be at a cost. Being special doesn't have to hurt.

## BE NICE TO YOURSELF

Ease up on yourself. Don't believe the garbage other people are saying *or* the garbage you may be telling yourself. You deserve to be believed—not just by other people, but by yourself too. So start believing in yourself. Take care of yourself. Be gentle with yourself. What you're going through is rough.

Okay, let's talk about what may be happening with you and your body now that the secret is out.

# 5

## What's Happening to Me?

*I felt like I was made of glass and could break into a million
pieces at any second. I couldn't eat, I felt wired all the
time; I didn't know what was going to happen to my life.*
BRYAN, SIXTEEN-YEAR-OLD ABUSED BY OLDER BROTHER

FTER YOU TELL about the abuse, you will most likely
enter what's called the "Emergency Stage." It's a very tough
place to be—but it's not forever.

You may feel like you are going nuts because people are
telling you that you must have misunderstood what happened or that
you're emotionally unstable. You may start questioning yourself and
whether you really were abused. You may find that all you can think
about or even talk about is the abuse. You may just want everybody to
shut up about the whole thing and forget it.

Now that it's out in the open, all your worst fears may be coming
true. People may be calling you a liar; your mother or the person who
should have protected you may be falling apart at the seams; your
brothers and sisters and other family members may be pressuring you
to say you were making the whole thing up; and you or the abuser may
have had to leave the house. Life may really stink right now.

Hang on. Remember, the decision to tell was a decision that you
made for yourself and for your future. You decided that you wanted to

heal, that you are valuable and have a right to a life free from abuse. You did the right thing, no matter what anybody else is saying to you. Telling about the abuse was a courageous act—and it will take all the guts you've got to stick to your story in the midst of all this tumult.

## DEALING WITH YOUR BODY'S REACTIONS

Right now, you may feel like a total wreck. You may be scared and anxious. You may feel like you have a label in the middle of your fore-head: "V" for "victim" or "I" for "incest." No matter where you go, you may feel like people are looking at you and pointing. You may feel that everyone you meet knows what happened to you. You may be startled easily or feel very shaky. You may be jittery, scared, nervous. Maybe you can't sleep, or you sleep all the time; maybe you can't eat, or you eat all the time. A zillion things may be going on inside you and none of them are making you feel very wonderful. Let's see if we can deal with some of the stuff that may be happening to you.

### SLEEPING

Your sleeping patterns may be all mixed up. You may find it hard to get to sleep at night and then next to impossible to get out of bed in the morning. You may be having nightmares or even be doing some sleepwalking. If that's the case, sleep may have become an enemy; going to sleep is too scary; you don't know what will happen in your dreams. Or it may be that your life feels totally out of control and sleep is the ultimate form of not being in control, so you avoid it.

On the other hand, you may want to sleep all the time. You may find yourself nodding off in class, in front of the TV, at the dinner table. For you, sleep has become an escape, a way to avoid the upheaval in your life, a way to shut out the nasty comments and pain.

Getting enough sleep, restful sleep, is going to be really important right now. You need to maintain your health.

If all else fails, see your doctor. She may be able to give you some mild medication or have some other suggestions that will help. Try some of the suggestions on the next page.

---

*HERE ARE SOME THINGS TO TRY WHEN YOU'RE HAVING TROUBLE GETTING TO SLEEP:*

1. *Intentionally relax your entire body. Start at your head and work your way down. Tighten each part and then release. Imagine all the tension leaving that part of your body when you release.*

2. *Play soothing music or environmental sounds like ocean waves, bird calls, or frog sounds. There are a number of tapes and CDs you can purchase.*

3. *Imagine yourself in a safe place surrounded by people who will protect you from harm.*

4. *Concentrate on making your mind blank. Some people try imagining an empty room. Others think of a strong door that's keeping all thoughts away.*

---

## FOOD

You may find that you can't eat, that the thought of food makes you sick at your stomach. Every time you do try to eat, you may get a burning sensation in your chest or even throw up. You may stop eating or eat only tiny portions and start to lose weight. This is not good.

On the other hand, you may find a lot of comfort in food and start eating all the time. You may think the only way to deal with the loneliness you suddenly feel or the sense of being different is to feed yourself some cookies (or ice cream, or chips, or fries, or whatever). This isn't good, either.

Food, like sleep, is an important part of staying healthy right now. Don't let this situation go. Talk to someone about the eating problems you're having. Your doctor may be a good place to start. Don't have a doctor? Ask your teacher, your social worker, or the child protective services worker to recommend one.

## OTHER PHYSICAL SYMPTOMS

Stress can cause all kinds of unusual physical symptoms, so there may be a whole lot of weird things going on with your body right now. You may be losing hair; handfuls of it may be on the floor of the shower each day. Your gums may start to pull back from your teeth and they may bleed easily. You may have a rash or little bumps on different parts of your body. Your face may break out in a terminal case of acne.

Lots of these things are normal. However, if they're getting out of hand, if you haven't slept in three days, or you've gained six pounds in one week, or you can't keep anything in your stomach except liquids, get some professional attention. If you're not sure whether something is stress related or not, see your doctor or talk to your therapist. Between the two of them, they can help you with sleeping problems, eating problems, and any other things that are going on.

Take care of yourself. You've come so far. Don't give up now.

# DEALING WITH YOUR ANXIETY AND FEAR

You may be spending your days in total anxiety. You may feel edgy and irritable. It may be like a low-grade fever or a full-blown panic attack. This is not unusual.

A lot of things are changing in your life right now. The abuser may be living away from the family or you may be living away from the family. You may have to keep telling your story over and over again to police, social service people, the state's attorney, teachers, friends, and others; you may be under a lot of pressure to take back what you said about the abuser; you may be worried about what's going to happen to your family—all kinds of things can be changing and shifting and your life may look a whole lot different from the way it did even a few days ago.

## HANDLING PANIC ATTACKS

Sometimes fear can have a physical effect on the body. Suddenly, you feel like you can't breathe, your heart is racing, your hands are trembling, you begin to sweat, your chest feels tight, and you think you're going to pass out or die. This is a panic attack and you *can* survive it.

Life may seem out of control right now.

The most important thing to do for yourself during a panic attack is to breathe *slowly*. Force yourself to take a slow deep breath—it may not be a big one, your chest may feel like it can't expand enough to take a big breath—but still try to take just a slow breath. This will help stop hyperventilation (fast, shallow breathing) and will slow your heart down. Once you get your breathing under control, the other symptoms will begin to fade and you'll start to feel like yourself again.

Panic attacks can be very scary. They come out of nowhere. You don't have much, if any, warning that they will happen. If they're happening frequently, you may need to get some medical help to control them. Talk to your doctor about this and any other physical things that are happening to your body. Don't have a doctor? Get one. Your social worker may be able to help you find a doctor who is capable of dealing with victims in a respectful and compassionate manner.

## HANDLING THREATS FROM THE ABUSER

Sometimes abusers make threats to their victims about what will happen if they tell. The abuser may have threatened to hurt you or someone you care about. Or she may have threatened to kill herself if you tell. This may have pushed you right past "edgy" and straight into "terrified."

You don't have to be fearful of what the abuser may do. Threats of any kind are important information for the police or social services to know. If you haven't told anyone about these threats, do it now. Call your social worker or the youth services division of your police department and let them know about it. Ask them what they will do with the information and how they will make sure you are safe.

## DEALING WITH YOUR EMOTIONS

You may feel very unstable right now. Your emotions may be all over the map. You may be like a powder keg waiting for a match or you may feel like a chicken who wandered into a fox's den. Hang in there. Your emotions will eventually calm down.

### FEELING CONFUSED

> I don't know whether to be angry or not. I feel really con-
> fused. Everybody tells me different things.
> DAVID, SIXTEEN-YEAR-OLD ABUSED BY HIS MOTHER

One of the most difficult things to deal with during the Emergency Stage is the total confusion you may be feeling. Some people may be giving you a lot of advice about what to say and do. Others may be telling you to act like nothing ever happened and just get on with your life.

You may be experiencing strong feelings of guilt because your family is in a lot of pain. You may be worried all the time about your parent or guardian who was not involved in the abuse because she is so upset about what has happened. Or you may feel discounted because the nonoffending parent won't deal with the abuse and acts as if it's no big thing.

You may have a lot of mixed emotions about the abuser. One fifteen-year-old girl told me, "I still love him and everything, but I don't want to talk to him." You may be wondering how the abuser is doing; is he scared? worried? sorry? angry? You may want to tell the abuser you still love him but are afraid to say it because the abuser may think that the abuse was no big deal. Or you may be absolutely furious with the abuser and wouldn't care a fig if he dropped dead tomorrow. Or you may have a combination of these feelings.

Life can seem pretty overwhelming about now. The first thing to remember is that you are not nuts or crazy and that all of your feelings are okay and normal. The second thing to remember is that you did the right thing by telling, even though you may be getting a lot of heat for doing it. The third thing to remember is that this is not going to last forever. The Emergency Stage with all its confusing emotions is a *stage*, a period of time with a beginning and end. *And you will survive it!*

## FEELING DEPRESSED

> Depression makes me crazy. It comes so long after the Incident that I can't figure out why I'm depressed. Like, if I have a fight with my boyfriend, one week later, I'll feel depressed.
>
> YVONNE, SIXTEEN-YEAR-OLD ABUSED BY UNCLE

Depression is often a part of being a teenager. However, you may be experiencing something more intense than the normal run-of-the-mill teenage depression.

Listed below are a number of symptoms of depression. If you have several of these symptoms, you may be depressed. If you have most of these symptoms, you should seek some help dealing with your depression.

## SIGNS OF DEPRESSION

- Do you have difficulty falling asleep?

- Do you have difficulty waking up no matter how much sleep you got during the night?

- Do you feel tired and without energy most of the time?

- Do you feel like you are living life through a fog or that everything takes a lot of effort?

- Are you having trouble concentrating and remembering things?

- What's happening to your grades? Are they going down? Have you had to drop out of classes or school activities?

- What's happening with your friends? Do you still see them a lot or are you spending more and more time by yourself?

- Are you crying a lot? Do you cry at the drop of a hat over things that ordinarily wouldn't upset you?

- Are you irritable? Do you feel like smacking people because you don't like the way they are breathing? Are you freaking out and getting angry over really little things?

- How do you feel about the future? Are you looking forward to events or could you care less what happens tomorrow?

- What do you look like? Have you taken a bath or a shower recently? (Last Wednesday is not recently.) Do you need a haircut? A shave? Are you wearing clean clothes? How do you smell? Are you taking care of yourself or are you letting yourself go?

- Are you being really clumsy lately? Are you falling over your own feet, getting into accidents with your car or your bike? Are you falling down a lot?

- Are you getting a lot of stomachaches? Headaches? Got any rashes or patches of itchy skin?

- Can you make decisions? We're not talking, "Should I be a brain surgeon or nuclear physicist?"; we're talking, "What movie should I go to?" or "Do I want mushrooms or pepperoni on my pizza?"

- Are you spending a lot of time thinking about death? Do you think about suicide? Have you been fantasizing about your funeral and how sorry everyone would be that you were dead?

This list may not cover everything that is happening to you. But it is a good measuring stick for whether or not depression is dragging you down.

Sometimes depression can be pretty severe and require strong measures to be corrected. If you find that depression is a continual problem, take care of yourself and get some help. Talk to a therapist; talk to your doctor; talk to someone. Don't let the depression get out of hand.

### You May Need Medical Help for Depression

Because depression can sometimes be caused by a chemical imbalance in your body, you may need to talk to your doctor about it. There are several different medications that doctors can prescribe to help combat depression that is caused by stress or depression that has resulted from a chemical mix-up in your body.

It's important to remember that alcohol and drugs are not going to cure your depression. In fact, they can make it worse. There are some medications that can help depression, but they must always be prescribed by a licensed physician, not bought on the street or taken from Mom and Dad's medicine cabinet.

You don't have to live in a depressed state. Doctors and therapists know that depression is a disease with a cause and a solution. So get the help you need; there's too much of life out there for you to miss it.

Don't be afraid to seek medical help.

### FEELING DESPERATE

*Some days I would like to just walk out of my life.*
AMBER, FIFTEEN-YEAR-OLD ABUSED BY STEPFATHER

*I wish I could fall asleep and never wake up.*
MICHAEL, FOURTEEN-YEAR-OLD ABUSED BY GRANDFATHER

You may be feeling very desperate during the Emergency Stage. You may feel nuts, alone, crazy, disgusting, dirty, a troublemaker, and like the world would be a better place without you in it. *Stop!*

*Do not hurt yourself.* You may have started or continued self-mutilation (cutting, burning, pinching, or otherwise hurting your own body). *Don't do it.* You don't deserve to be hurt anymore—not by yourself or anyone else.

You may have begun to think about ways to kill yourself because that seems the only way to end all the pain you're feeling. *Don't do it.* If you're feeling suicidal right now, go to Chapter Nine and read "Suicide" or turn to page 68 for words of encouragement from other survivors. Just *don't hurt yourself.*

One way to deal with desperation is to make a "Blues Buster" list. This is a list of all the things you can do for yourself when you are feeling blue or down. Do them before the blues turn into desperation or suicidal thoughts. Here are a few suggestions:

1. Take several deep breaths and relax your body from head to toe.

2. Find a rocking chair in a safe place and sit down and rock—as slowly or quickly as you want.

3. Pet a cat or dog or a stuffed animal.

4. Do something energetic: ride a bike, play soccer or basketball, go roller-blading, take a run, jump rope, hit a punching bag.

5. Call your social worker or a "buddy" (someone who has agreed to be available whenever you need to talk).

6. Listen to music, but only the kind that will lift your spirits, like pop, disco, spiritual. No suicidal lyrics.

7. Pamper your body: give your-  self a facial, take a hot bubble bath or a long hot shower, deep condition your hair.

8. Watch reruns of your favorite comedy show—and laugh.

9. Make plans for some future event, like a day of hiking or biking or a weekend of camping—something you will look forward to.

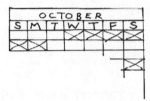

10. Work on something soothing, like a favorite hobby (woodworking, sewing, macrame, bird watching).

11. Do whatever releases your stress in a healthy way: murdering someone is not the answer.

12. Do the things on this list over and over until you have busted the blues.

Make up your own list of Blues Busters and keep it handy.

**Don't Let Desperation Get Out of Control**

Get some help. Call someone: a suicide hot line, a friend, a teacher, a social worker, your parent(s). You'd be surprised how many people out there care about you and your well-being. There is help and comfort for you out there—you just have to reach out for it. Please, please don't hurt yourself.

## WORDS OF ENCOURAGEMENT

The following statements are from real live people who have been sexually abused and are working to move on with their lives. These statements are from survivors who range in age from fifteen years old to the mid twenties.

You *can* heal.

TWENTY-SIX-YEAR-OLD SURVIVOR

There is hope.

TWENTY-SIX-YEAR-OLD SURVIVOR

You are not alone. There are a lot of us out here.

TWENTY-FOUR-YEAR-OLD SURVIVOR

It's going to be really hard, but it's worth it.

SIXTEEN-YEAR-OLD SURVIVOR

You are not permanently damaged.

TWENTY-SIX-YEAR-OLD SURVIVOR

You're going to be okay.

EIGHTEEN-YEAR-OLD SURVIVOR

It's worth going on.

NINETEEN-YEAR-OLD SURVIVOR

Find someone safe to go through this with.

NINETEEN-YEAR-OLD SURVIVOR

Hang on.

NINETEEN-YEAR-OLD SURVIVOR

Don't let people discourage you.

FIFTEEN-YEAR-OLD SURVIVOR

I would rather talk to a million people about it than go through the abuse again.

SEVENTEEN-YEAR-OLD SURVIVOR

Once you tell, you stop being a victim—you have power.

SEVENTEEN-YEAR-OLD SURVIVOR

Always remember, it's not your fault.

SIXTEEN-YEAR-OLD SURVIVOR

The fact that you've been hurt doesn't make you any less of a person.

EIGHTEEN-YEAR-OLD SURVIVOR

I respect you.

FIFTEEN-YEAR-OLD SURVIVOR

# 6

## Living with Your Family Now That You've Told

*I'm really mad at my family for not being there for me. Why did Mom let him back in again? They knew he was sick but didn't do anything about it. I was the one who had to pay the price for their stupidity.*

KATHERINE, SIXTEEN-YEAR-OLD ABUSED BY BIOLOGICAL FATHER

THIS CHAPTER IS ABOUT FAMILIES and their response to finding out that someone in the family has been sexually abused. Revelations of sexual abuse can be an explosion in a family. All of a sudden the family has to look at itself in a different way: maybe they're not the wholesome happy family they thought they were; maybe the entire picture of the family has been a lie.

You too will have to take a closer look at your family now that the abuse is out in the open. You'll need to figure out how you feel about these people whom you are supposed to love. You may have a lot more feelings of anger and rage right now than you do of love. You may also have to face up to some feelings of grief in realizing that your family isn't what you wanted it to be.

Let's begin sorting this out by looking at how families respond to revelations of abuse.

# YOUR FAMILY'S RESPONSE TO THE TELLING OF THE SECRET

The way everyone reacts when someone says, "Hey, something really bad has happened to me" will vary from family to family. One of the things that makes a difference in a family's reaction is who the abuser is. If the abuser is outside the family, then everyone may deal with the revelation a little bit better than if the abuser is a family member.

## WHEN THE ABUSER IS OUTSIDE THE FAMILY

If the abuser is not a member of the family or a close family friend, the members of your family may have an easier time believing and dealing with your claim of abuse. It's a lot easier to believe that the abuser is the babysitter or a boy scout leader than if it's Daddy or Aunt Louise.

This doesn't mean that your family isn't going to go through an earthquake when you tell about the abuse; most likely they will. It just may not be as big an earthquake as it would be if the person who abused you was a member of the family.

### How Your Parents May React

When your parents hear that someone has sexually abused you, they may say, "I can't believe it" or "Why didn't you tell us?" Parents are not intentionally trying to be insensitive; they are just totally unprepared. Your parents may feel disbelief, anger, guilt, stress. They may ask themselves, "How could this have happened?" "Where were we?" "How could we not have protected our child?"

Fathers who are not abusers will often feel a very strong desire to "beat the geek" out of the offender. It can be especially hard for dads because they believe they are supposed to keep their families safe. When they find out that something bad has happened to their child, dads may become depressed and feel like they are lesser men.

Mothers who are not abusers can also suffer from depression. It's very hard to know that someone has hurt your child, maybe even someone you trusted with your child or with whom you encouraged your child to spend time.

> **Your parents may get caught up in their own emotions and not see how much you need them. Don't be afraid to say, "Please comfort me" or, "I need you, Mom and Dad."**

Parents can get caught in the guilt grip: "Why didn't I know? Why didn't I see it? Why didn't I listen to him when he said he didn't want to go to that school anymore?" Concern about their guilt can sometimes get in the way of your parents' ability to deal effectively with you and your emotions. Parents can sometimes spend so much time beating themselves up over what they think is their failure as a parent that they can't see what you're going through. You may have to point it out. As always, try to do so in a way that they can hear. If you yell and scream and swear, they're going to shut you out. If you, as calmly as possible, try to tell them you really need them to be there for you, most nonabusing parents will do their best to attend to your needs.

On the other hand, there are parents who will not believe you, who will tell you you imagined it, misunderstood what happened, or are lying. It's hard to deal with a parent's denial. Nobody likes to be called a liar or told he has an overactive imagination, especially when he knows he's telling the truth. Stay firm in what you know happened. Don't give up because people are having difficulty understanding that you were abused. Stick with what you know to be true. After all, you know what happened; you were there.

### How Your Brothers and Sisters May React

When you reveal that you have been abused by someone outside your family, your brothers and sisters (like all your relatives) may have an easier time believing you than if you had been abused by a member of your family. They may be angry and indignant that you were abused. They may stick up for you when people ask prying questions. They may be supportive and protective.

On the other hand, your sisters and brothers may be very upset by your claims of abuse. They may hate what the revelation has done to their lives. If the abuser is someone prominent in the community, there may be a lot of publicity about the abuse. Your brothers and sisters may really despise the invasion of their privacy and may blame you.

Brothers and sisters may also get upset with the attention you're getting. Even if the abuser is not someone well known in your community, there may still be many people who are expressing concern about your welfare. Additionally, your parents may be really tied up with you right now. They may be taking you from interviews with the police to appointments with a therapist to meetings with lawyers. Your parents may not have a lot of time for your siblings and your brothers and sisters may resent it.

Remember that your brothers and sisters (as well as the rest of your family) are *choosing* how to respond to the abuse. You are not responsible for their actions and words and you don't have to put up with a lot of anger being dumped on you.

At the same time, try to remember that this is a tough period for everyone in your family. No one may be coping very well with the revelation, so give people a little slack, if you can.

## WHEN THE ABUSER IS A MEMBER OF THE FAMILY

The closer your family is to the offender, the harder it will be for them to believe you. If your father's best friend, the guy he's known since second grade, is the abuser, you can imagine how difficult it's going to be for your dad to come to grips with this. If it's your older brother who can do no wrong and has a brilliant athletic career ahead of him, then it's going to be real hard for your parents (and other members of the family) to cope with your accusations.

And if the abuser is your father, your stepfather, or your mom's boyfriend, then step back: telling about the abuse is going to cause an explosion in your family.

### How the Nonoffending Parent May React

The nonoffending parent is the parent who did not abuse you. If you were abused by your mom, then your father is the nonoffending parent. If you were abused by your dad, then your mom is the nonoffending parent. If you were abused by a brother or sister, an uncle, grandparent, or other relative, then both of your parents are nonoffending parents.

Let's say the abuser was your stepfather. This is going to be a major blast to your mother's life and everything she has believed in. Think about it. If she believes you, then she has to disbelieve everything she knows about her husband. Her trust in him has been violated also.

She's going to want to deny your claim at first because to accept what you say means that she has to look at this person in a whole different way. She has to forget all the good times—the love they share, the intimacies—and see him as a child molester. Not an easy thing to do.

She is going to have to question her own judgment in making a commitment to this person. Sexual abusers do not wear a sign or have a special mark, so there are a lot of people out there who are finding out the partners they are involved with are not all they thought they were. But your mom is not going to think that she has lots of company. At first she's going to feel very isolated, very alone. She's going to feel like she can't tell anyone—it's too horrible. (Bet you can relate to that!)

She may want to convince you that it wasn't as bad as you thought, and can't you just forget about it and let it alone. Or worse, she may not be able to believe you at all. She may tell you that he would never do anything like that, that he is a fine upstanding man, maybe even a churchgoer. How could you tell lies like this?

Remember, your mom is trying to deal with the explosion that just happened in her life. Her initial denial is her coping mechanism for dealing with this bomb in her life—and be assured: this will be a bomb.

If the abuser was someone other than a parent, let's say your uncle or your grandfather, both of your parents will probably still have a

hard time dealing with your revelation. They won't want to believe
that a member of the family could be a child molester. They also may
not want to face up to some abuse in their own childhood by that
same abuser.

Yep, that's right. Abuse can travel down the generations of families.
If your grandfather abused you, then there's a chance he may have
abused his own children, your mom or dad. If your cousin abused you,
it's possible that he or she was abused by someone else in the family.
Abuse can be a chain reaction, like dominoes, with the same effect:
everybody falls down.

### How the Rest of Your Family May React

Have you ever been with a friend who started acting weird or who
looked a mess or who did something wrong? How did you feel when
you were with that friend? Did you feel responsible? Were you afraid
that everyone else would think that you were weird too? Did you
worry that you might be accused of the wrongdoing?

Well, it's no different for a family who has a member who is a sexual offender. When the abuser is someone inside the family, family members are often afraid that the abuser's actions will be a reflection on them, so they feel a strong urge to deny or disbelieve.

Your other relatives may be very unsupportive right now. They do not want to be associated with things like sexual abuse, incest, child molester, victim, the law. Your brothers and sisters may be putting the heat on you to "keep your mouth shut" because they're too embarrassed for their friends to know what the abuser did.

Your grandparents may be pretending they don't even know you or that they always knew you were a troublemaker. They don't want to believe that someone in their family, maybe even their own child, is a sex offender.

The rest of your relatives may be choosing sides. And not many may be choosing your side. This is hard. Find people who will support you—people like your therapist, members of a survivors' group, friends, other adults in your life.

## WHY DIDN'T SOMEONE PROTECT ME?

There is usually someone who the victim of sexual abuse feels should have protected him or her from the abuser. That person might be a grandmother, a mother, an older brother, or an adult friend. The point is that there is probably someone in your life who you felt should have kept you safe.

If you were sexually abused by your father, stepfather, foster father, or mother's boyfriend, then you probably expected your mother to protect you from the abuse. If you were abused by your mother, grandparent, or uncle, you may have looked to your father to protect you. If you were abused by someone outside your family, then it's possible that you expected both your mother and your father to keep you from harm.

If both your parents, or the adults in your life who were in a parental role (foster parents, relatives you lived with, or others) were abusing you, then you may never have felt like there was anyone in your life who should have or could have protected you. Unfortunately, cases of ritualistic and satanic abuse can involve both parents, so the victim feels like there is no one whom they can turn to, who could protect them.

The most important thing to remember in discussing the person you think should have protected you is that he or she was not responsible for the abuse. Remember: the abuser is the only one responsible for the abuse. That doesn't mean that you can't be angry at your "protector" for not keeping you safe or picking up on the hints that you may have been dropping. It doesn't mean that you can't be angry at your "protector" for being unresponsive to you or maybe abusing you physically or verbally. It also doesn't mean that you can't be angry that your "protector" may have been weak or a doormat. These are pretty normal feelings among kids who are sexually abused.

What it *does* mean is that you can't blame your "protector" for the abuse. (Obviously, if your "protector" held you down while you were abused, or knowingly set you up, then he or she should be held responsible for that part of the abuse.)

Most sexually abused kids look to their mothers as their protector IF their mother was not the one who abused them. Most kids also have a whole lot of anger at their mom for failing to take care of them and keep them safe.

> *Remember: even though you may be really angry with the person or persons who did not protect you, they are still not responsible for the abuse. The abuser is always responsible.*

## WHERE WAS MOM?

When a mother first hears that her child was sexually abused, she may get mad, defensive, or call her child a liar. But eventually, most moms ask themselves, "Where was I? How could I not have known?"

### I Didn't Know

Mothers frequently haven't a clue that abuse is happening. They really have no inkling that their child is being hurt.

> I had no idea that this was happening. I thought me [sic]
> and my husband were doing fine.
>
> GLORY, MOTHER OF THIRTEEN-YEAR-OLD DAUGHTER

As you know, abusers are very careful about guarding the secret. They can be very tricky and sly about the way they abuse a child. So old Mom gets left out in the cold about a lot of stuff. She may see that her son doesn't want to spend any time with his father or that her daughter becomes very upset when she's left alone at home with older brother. But moms generally don't know what to make of this. A lot of times they'll figure it's just hormones and that "teenage stuff."

## I Knew Something Was Wrong

Mothers of sexually abused kids often say that they knew something was wrong, but they didn't know what. They feel a tension, a stress in the family, but they can't identify it.

> I knew that something was wrong. I just had this feeling . . .
> but I didn't know what was wrong. I saw a couple of odd
> things, but I blamed everything on his drinking.
>
> DEBBIE, MOTHER OF ELEVEN-YEAR-OLD AND
> THIRTEEN-YEAR-OLD DAUGHTERS

When they can't put a label on what's causing the tension, moms will often push their worry aside or tell themselves they're imagining things or find some other type of explanation.

> My husband is very inward and my daughter was acting
> the same way. We had marriage problems and I just
> thought it was her way of dealing with it.
>
> ABBY, MOTHER OF TWELVE-YEAR-OLD DAUGHTER

## I Didn't Want to See It

There are some mothers who do know about the abuse; they've seen the blood on their son's sheets and the redness of his backside. Or they've had to take their daughter to the doctor because she has a venereal disease. These mothers have real evidence that something isn't right, that someone is harming their child, but they look the other way because they simply cannot deal with what is happening.

I didn't want to see it.

Hindsight is always 20/20. Looking back now, I can see that some of the things I chose to believe were okay or "normal" really weren't. I'd like to plead total ignorance, but the truth is, there was a piece of me that knew. And, God forgive me, I didn't have the guts to do anything about it.

LEAH, MOTHER OF FOURTEEN-YEAR-OLD SON ABUSED BY STEPFATHER

When a mother begins to process the idea that her child is being sexually abused, she starts looking at the impact this will have on her life. If her husband or boyfriend is the abuser, not only is she dealing with her own sense of being played for a fool but she also has to take a hard look at what throwing the abuser out will do to her life.

For some moms, that's their first reaction—get rid of him. But then they take a look at what getting rid of him will mean. If mom is financially dependent on the abuser, this is going to be really difficult. She may decide that she literally can't afford to get rid of the abuser and will decide to look the other way or encourage you to forget about the abuse if you've told.

For other moms, recognizing that their child is being sexually abused may force them to look at some abuse in their own lives. It may be that along with sexually abusing you, Dad is also abusing Mom, and she can't face up to her own abuse, let alone yours.

It could be that your mother was herself sexually abused as a child. To deal with your being abused may mean that she has to deal with her own abuse and she simply can't.

There are a lot of reasons many moms look the other way and pretend that everything is fine.

# GETTING ALONG
# WITH MOM . . .

*I could never do anything well enough for my mother. I never
felt like she was proud of me or glad that I was her daughter.*
LYNN, SEVENTEEN-YEAR-OLD ABUSED BY BIOLOGICAL FATHER

Whether you hated your mother, longed for her approval, or pitied
her, you probably did not have a close, loving relationship with her.
Most victims of sexual abuse talk about tension between themselves
and their mothers. Many never felt they could talk to their mothers
about really important things like feelings or sexual abuse.

Some mothers don't know how to have a close relationship with
their children. They didn't have one with their parents and have no
idea how to create one with their own children. Other mothers feel
unable to deal with trouble. They see their child pulling away or
becoming withdrawn but don't know what to do about it.

Whatever your relationship was with your mother prior to the
abuse, you have a chance to establish a new, better relationship now
that she knows about the abuse. Granted, it may not work in all cases;
some mothers will never believe what you have to say. If that's your situation, it's not easy. In fact, having your mother, of all people, not
believe you and take the side of the abuser can be devastating. It can
feel almost as bad as the abuse; it's another betrayal.

If your mother (or protector) won't believe you, it *is* possible to find
another adult who will. That adult can be an ally, supporter, encour-
ager, nurturer—all the things that you need right now. It may take
some hard work to find an adult like that, but it's necessary as well as
worth it. Some kids find that a teacher, social worker, therapist, or
friend's mother can do this job.

But for those whose mothers (or protectors) are willing at least to
listen and try to deal with the fact of the abuse, there is hope that a
new and better relationship can occur. It requires some effort,
though, on your part as well as your mother's. Things between you
may look very different from before. A lot of things are changing
right now in *both* your lives, and these changes can cause a lot of
difficulties between you.

It may be helpful if you and your mom consider getting some therapy together. Your social worker or child protective services worker can help you find out what is available to you, especially what may be available to you free. Since you are the victim of a crime, you may be eligible for some free counseling through the Victims of Crime Act (VOCA). You won't know until you ask about it, so ask. (For more on VOCA and how to find a therapist, see Chapter Eight.)

## DEALING WITH YOUR MOM'S RESPONSE

The first thing you may have to do to build a better relationship with your mom is to sort out your feelings about her response when you told her about the abuse. Her initial reaction may have been less than wonderful.

> My mother called me a whore and told me that if her boyfriend did anything to me, it was my own fault.
> STACY, FIFTEEN-YEAR-OLD ABUSED BY MOTHER'S BOYFRIEND

Some mothers say it without thinking, but then the more they listen to what their child is saying, the more they begin to believe.

> I needed a lot of clarification before I could believe my son. I wanted to be sure that there wasn't any misunderstanding, so I asked him a lot of questions. Part of me wanted so much to believe that the facts weren't straight.
> SANDY, MOTHER OF ELEVEN-YEAR-OLD BOY ABUSED BY
> HER HUSBAND

Other moms call their child a liar and keep right on doing it all the way through the telling, the social workers, the legal system, and court.

> We're sitting there in court and my mother keeps saying that I'm just saying all this stuff because I want attention. Like this is really the kind of attention I want.
> MELINDA, FIFTEEN-YEAR-OLD ABUSED BY STEPFATHER

It may feel like it's impossible to create a new relationship with a mom who is this disbelieving—and it may be. The only way to find out for sure is to give it a try.

On the other hand, your mom may have a wonderful response to your telling. She may believe you, she may put the abuser out of the house, she may get you professional attention. But then she falls apart.

> I believed her right away. But I fell apart when the doctor confirmed it. In my mind, I was really hoping someone would come in and say it was all a mistake.
> EILEEN, MOTHER OF THIRTEEN-YEAR-OLD ABUSED BY HUSBAND

All your hopes of surviving the revelation may be dashed by your mom's falling apart. You may be angry at her that she's not being strong and taking care of you; you may feel guilty because she is so distressed; you may feel betrayed: you thought you could trust her belief and here she is having a nervous breakdown. Try to hang in there if you can. This is a very hard time for your mom. She may be able to pull it back together and you can start finding ways to get along.

You may find that counseling is the best place for you and your mom to try to reestablish a relationship. Your feelings about each other may be too intense for you to sort out on your own. If that's your case, then the smart thing would be to talk to your mom about finding a therapist or seeing what is available for you through your social services department.

Some kids are able to work through the difficulties with their moms on their own. However, this is successful only when both mom and teen are willing to make a go of it, to listen to each other carefully, to stop blaming each other for what happened, and to put the blame where it belongs (if you said the blame belongs with the abuser, you get 300 points), and to try again and again. Like everything else with sexual abuse, none of this is easy, but it is possible.

> A lot of times you need encouragement from your mother but she just won't believe you. Understand, that even if she never believes you, life goes on.
> GAYLE, A TWENTY-YEAR-OLD SURVIVOR

There's nothing I can say that will take away the pain of being called a liar, a whore, an attention seeker, or all of the other horrible things that mothers can say. I can only remind you that *you* are the one who knows what really happened and who the abuser really is. It took a lot of courage to tell. It will take a lot of courage to hang tough in the face of disbelief—especially a mother's disbelief.

## OVERCOMING OLD HABITS

If you and your mother are committed to reworking your relationship, then the next issue you may have to deal with is the ways you used to interact, the old habits.

> My mother expects me to relate to her in the old ways. When I try to be different, it causes problems. And I end up feeling taken advantage of.
> ANITA, SEVENTEEN-YEAR-OLD ABUSED BY STEPFATHER

During the abuse, the stress you were under most likely was reflected in your relationship with your mother. Perhaps you were rude or were sulky with her. You may have treated her like an idiot or a know-nothing. Now that the abuse is out in the open, you may feel that there is no reason for you to continue treating your mother the way you did. You may be hopeful that you and Mom will now no longer fight about clothes, argue about curfews, or disagree about the appropriateness of co-ed sleepovers. You may be looking forward to being your mother's friend.

Mom, on the other hand, may have come to expect nothing but rudeness, bad moods, and a superior attitude from you; no matter what you do or say, she hears it through the old filter.

You and your mom may be locked into a style of interacting that is not healthy for either one of you and it may take time, energy, and some outside help to break the old habits and begin a new way of relating to one another.

## OVERCOMING YOUR MOM'S RESENTMENT

> My mother makes me nuts. The whole time my father was sexually abusing me, he put me in a higher position than my mother. He always treated me special. Now, I feel like my mom is getting back at me for that.
> KARLA, FIFTEEN-YEAR-OLD ABUSED BY STEPFATHER

If you are a girl abused by your father, stepfather or mother's boyfriend, you may find yourself in the unfortunate position of being "the other woman," the person who is blamed for coming between your mother and father.

This "other woman" stuff is garbage. You weren't responsible for what happened, but your mother may not see it that way. In fact, she may have real difficulty viewing you as the victim. She may take that label for herself and call you a slut, whore, home wrecker, or any other number of horrid things.

Your mother may not be able to view you as her daughter but only as competition. You are younger, your body is firmer and without stretch marks, your skin is unwrinkled, and your future is still before you. Your mother, no matter how hard she tries to push it down, may feel very strong resentment toward you.

Is this fair? No! Is this reasonable? No! Is it a normal response? Yes! Does it happen a lot? Yes!

Therapy is the place you and your mom can find help in sorting out this aspect of your relationship. No matter how bad things seem right now, if your mother is willing to get into therapy with you, then there's a good chance that you will be able to build a new and better relationship.

## OVERCOMING YOUR RESISTANCE TO CHANGING ROLES

> After I told about the abuse, my mother suddenly became a mother and not the child. She used to be the kid and I was the parent. It was really hard when that changed.
> MARTY, SIXTEEN-YEAR-OLD ABUSED BY STEPFATHER

Some kids are really the parents in their households. They take responsibility for household chores. They take care of younger siblings. They keep at least one of their parents happy. Girls as well as guys may find that they have been viewed as another adult in the household by one or both of their parents.

When the abuse is revealed and the family begins to find new ways of looking at each other, you may lose your place as an adult. While that position had a lot of negativity associated with it and a lot of stress, it may also have given you some freedoms that many of your friends may not have enjoyed.

Now that status may be changing and you may not like it. If your mother was always in bed with a sick headache while you did laundry, paid bills, and watched the younger children, it may not be easy to start seeing your mother in a strong parental role. Or if your father was always meek and acted like a doormat while your mother treated you like her lover, you may have a hard time seeing him stand up and be counted once the abuse is revealed.

Things are going to change, and that's not necessarily bad. However, you may find that you and your mother can not begin a new relationship without some help. If you are involved in a social services system, you may have counseling available to you and your mom. This can be very helpful. Sometimes it's easier to talk about the abuse and your relationship with each other when there is a third person (the counselor or social worker) sitting in the room.

If you're not involved with social services, then you and your mother might consider getting some help from a private therapist who has experience in the field of sexual abuse and incest.

Therapy can help, but there's no guarantee that you will be able to work out a new and better relationship with the person you wanted to protect you. In fact, one seventeen-year-old told me, "Sometimes to

Therapy may help build new relationships.

heal a severed relationship, it's best to cut it off." That may very well be how things work out for you. But you won't know that until you've first tried to put it back together.

## WHAT ONE MOTHER HAS TO SAY

Following is a letter written by a mother whose daughter was sexually abused by her biological father. This mom is pretty courageous about showing her feelings—the good and the bad—as well as sharing some of the struggle she and her daughter have had in learning to get along. This letter may not be a reflection of what you are experiencing with your mom, but it shows that moms and their abused kids can find common ground, peace, and even love after the telling.

> Dearest Daughter,
> I remember that day as if it were yesterday. When I came home to pick you up, I could see the hatred in your eyes. My blood began to boil when you told me what your father had done again.
> All I wanted to do was kill him. But what good would I be to you if I were in jail? I hated your father for what he did to you and myself for letting him.
> I was so scared. I was feeling very insecure about myself and at the same time trying to keep us together. I didn't like being away from you for that week we were apart; having to tell people about our so-called perfect family. What a joke!
> I was so angry at your father I felt like I could bust inside.
> I knew you didn't want to go into any kind of group [therapy] at this time. But I know you are glad that you did. I began a mothers' group not long after that.
> I can't believe how far I have come. During the first two years, I was confused, frightened, and sometimes lost in my own world. But we have helped each other through those tough times. We have learned to communicate [with] each other without fighting like we used to do.

Honey, it has been three years now since the disclosure of the abuse. I love you just as much today, if not more, as I did that day it came out.

We have our spats but I feel that we have worked them out the best way we know how. I have watched and helped you grow into a lovely young woman. I tried to be your friend instead of your mother and that is not what you were looking for. I have learned to talk to you through my feelings, which is very hard for me. But I am working on this.

I love the way you express your feelings and how I feel you stand your ground. I hope I get there someday. I know you need your space and I hope I give it to you. . . . I'm thankful that you now come to me when you have a problem. I now put myself in your place and try to help the best way I can by talking to you instead of brushing you off.

You have made me very happy. I'm proud of you.

Love,
Mom

# 7

## Going to Court

*Court is going to be hell — but it's worth it.*
AMBER, FIFTEEN-YEAR-OLD ABUSED BY HER STEPFATHER

WHEN ABUSE IS REVEALED, there is a good chance that the victim will have to go to court, to face the abuser and tell the world what happened. For a lot of kids, this is their worst nightmare and it's one of the many reasons they don't tell anyone about the abuse. Before you decide you're not going to tell because you don't want to end up in court, take some time to read this chapter. You may find that court isn't the "Nightmare on Main Street" that you thought it would be.

### WILL MY CASE HAVE TO GO TO COURT?

Not all cases of child sexual abuse end up in court. However, sexually abusing a child *is* a crime. It is a very serious offense and many reported cases do end up in court.

This does not always mean that *you* will end up in court. It could be that just the abuser does. There are a lot of considerations that go into the decision of whether a case or a victim goes to court.

It is important to remember that the laws and procedures for handling reports of sexual abuse vary from state to state. The following information is simply an example of what happens in some states. Your state may handle reports and court proceedings in a totally different manner, but this explanation will give you some idea of what goes into determining if a case will go to court.

## CAN THE CASE BE WON?

First, the prosecutor (that's the attorney who will be representing the state and who has the job of proving the abuse happened) must decide if she can win the case. Many times a victim's version of what happened is believed but other circumstances make the testimony confusing or impossible to prove. This could be because of the child's age, the prominence of the alleged offender within the community, or inconsistencies in the evidence.

### Prosecution Can Be Difficult for Young Victims

Often children who are very young, three or four years old, will say things that indicate they have been sexually abused, but because of their age, it is difficult to use them as witnesses. Instead of taking the case to court, the agencies involved may decide to use other methods to keep the child safe.

### Prosecution Can Be Difficult When the Abuser Is Well Known

Sometimes, the offender is someone very important within the community. It could be a doctor, a priest, or a teacher. When the report is made and investigated, the prosecutor has to consider that it may be difficult to dispel the "community leader" image of the offender and prove that what the twelve-year-old victim is saying is true. Proving it is not impossible, but determining whether it can be done in court is a part of the process that a prosecutor goes through in deciding whether she can take a case to court.

### Prosecution Can Be Difficult When There's Not Much Evidence

Evidence can be a very important piece of winning because cases of sexual abuse are tried in criminal court. This means that the prosecutor must prove "beyond a reasonable doubt" that the abuse did happen. The prosecutor's only evidence of what happened may be your testimony. She may not have any evidence like "the yellow rope he tied me up with is in the left-hand drawer of the bureau and the blue mask he wore is in the attic behind the Christmas decorations." There isn't usually hard evidence to show that abuse has occurred and in many cases it's the kid's word against the word of an adult, a situation that can make the whole thing an uphill battle.

### Preliminary Hearing or Grand Jury

Another step in the path of taking a case to court is the pretrial hearing. In order to charge a person with a felony, such as sexual abuse, the case has to be presented to a grand jury or to a judge at a preliminary hearing. The purpose of these types of hearings is to determine whether it is more likely than not that a crime was committed and that the person charged with the crime actually committed it. This means that before the *trial* to decide whether the abuser is guilty, there is a *hearing* to decide whether a trial should be held at all.

*Remember: the purpose of the grand jury or preliminary hearing is not to decide whether the abuser is guilty. It's to decide whether a criminal trial should be held at all.*

Some states have only preliminary hearings; some states have only a grand jury hearing; some states have both. A grand jury is made up of twenty-three citizens from the county where the abuse occurred. It will be the job of these folks to decide if it's more likely than not that a crime was committed. If they decide that it is more likely, then formal charges are made against the abuser and a trial date is set.

The grand jury hearing is held behind closed doors; the public is not allowed to be in the room during the proceedings. Additionally, the people testifying go in one at a time; you don't have the abuser, the police detective, the social worker, and all the other witnesses in the room at the same time. So if you have to testify at a grand jury hearing, there is a good chance that you won't have to face the abuser.

Other states don't use the grand jury, but instead have a preliminary hearing. Like the grand jury hearing, the purpose of a preliminary hearing is to gather information and see whether it is more likely than not that a crime was committed. Unlike the grand jury, however, the preliminary hearing does not have twenty-three citizens as the jurors. Only a judge hears the case at a preliminary hearing and he or she will make the decision about the likelihood that a crime has been committed.

Whether you will have to testify at a pretrial hearing is decided by the laws in your state and also by what the prosecutor believes is best for the case. However, the abuser is present in the courtroom during a preliminary hearing and will be there if you have to testify.

In some states, *hearsay* evidence is allowed into the record at a grand jury hearing or a preliminary hearing. Hearsay evidence is what someone knows because she was told about it, not because she witnessed it herself. This means that if you told a social worker or police detective about the abuse, he can relate that information to the grand jury or at a preliminary hearing. However, hearsay is not usually allowed in a criminal trial. Therefore, even though you may not have to testify at a grand jury hearing or a preliminary hearing, you may still have to testify at a criminal trial.

Ask the prosecutor or your social worker about your state's laws regarding testifying and whether you will have to testify at any pretrial hearings or at the trial itself.

## ABUSER'S RESPONSE TO THE CHARGES

Another factor in whether a case goes to court is the abuser's response to the charges of sexual abuse. If the abuser confesses and says, "Yes, she's telling the truth. I did those things," then court is not as big an issue. The abuser can simply plead guilty and be sentenced without you testifying. More frequently, however, abusers deny that they have done anything wrong and the issue of court looms large.

### Some Abusers Find Relief in Confessing

Some abusers may be glad that the problem is out in the open. The abuser may care enough about the victim not to argue or disagree with the victim's statement about the abuse.

> At first, my father said he didn't do it. Then he said he did. He seemed to realize for the first time what he had done. He got real suicidal and had to be in the hospital for three weeks.
>
> BUDDY, FIFTEEN-YEAR-OLD ABUSED BY BIOLOGICAL FATHER

The abuser may not wait for the authorities to come to him; he may make a confession and turn himself in. It doesn't happen often, but it *does* happen.

### Most Abusers Deny and Deny and Deny

Many abusers care more about sparing themselves than the victim. They can't even acknowledge to themselves how wrong they have been, so they give a different version of what happened. This type of abuser might want to present you as a liar and may suggest that you have always been a liar.

> To this day, my stepfather doesn't admit he did anything wrong. He lives in another country and I live with my Mom. Just last month, he calls me up and offers me a plane ticket so I could go live with him. He's on the phone saying, "I really, really love you. I don't understand why you said all those things. You can have a new bike, a TV, a cat, a horse." He knows I love animals, so he's bribing me. If I could have reached through the phone, I would have strangled him.
>
> MARISSA, FIFTEEN-YEAR-OLD ABUSED BY STEPFATHER

The abuser may twist what actually happened all around: instead of acknowledging that he initiated touching your breasts, he might say that you were the one to grab his hand and place it on your breasts.

Or the abuser may admit that he showed you his penis and asked you to take your clothes off so he could "check you out," but he says he did it as part of his responsibility to educate you about growing up and teach you about adult sexuality.

Then there are the "it was only an accident" kind of abusers. The abuser might admit that she touched you between your legs when you were wrestling with her on the floor, but will say that it was an accident and her hand just "slipped."

All these actions and statements are an attempt to dismiss responsibility. By using denial ("it never happened") or rationalization ("there was a good reason this happened") the abuser is trying to make himself or herself look better. When an abuser does this, it puts you in the position of having to present your version of what happened. This means that in order for you to be heard, and in order for the abuser to face consequences, you will most likely need to testify in court.

## YOUR WILLINGNESS TO TESTIFY

You, and your willingness or unwillingness to testify, are a major part of the decision about whether the case will go to court. It may be that the idea of going to court is the worst horror on the face of the earth for you. You may dread it more than anything else.

> When I found out that I would have to testify against my brother, I was so scared. I had horrible nightmares. The worst one was this dream I had over and over where the jury was throwing knives at me.
>
> BRYAN, SIXTEEN-YEAR-OLD ABUSED BY OLDER BROTHER

### I Don't Want to Testify

You may feel that you are being forced by other people to go public and reveal the most secret parts of your life. You may be feeling terror at the thought of being in the same room with the abuser. It may be that you simply cannot face testifying in court. If that is your position, then the prosecutor must decide how strong the case is without your testimony. It's possible that there isn't any case without your taking the stand and that the abuser will go free. That thought may help you reconsider your position.

If you still can't deal with testifying, then let it go. Don't even think about beating yourself up because you don't want to testify. And don't buy into other people's pressure because you've decided not to testify. The bottom line is that you must take care of *you*, and if testifying is more than you can handle, then that's how it is. Give it careful consideration and respect yourself and whatever decision you make about it.

### I Can't Wait to Testify

On the other hand, this may be the moment you have waited for—a chance to tell your own version of what happened, to see the abuser squirm and endure the consequences of what he's done. You may be beating down the prosecutor's door with your enthusiasm for going to court and having a chance to take the stand. Your testimony could make your case stronger and more easily won.

### You Get to Decide How You Feel About Testifying

There's no right or wrong way to feel about going to court and testifying. Your emotions may be taking you all over the place; you may be uneasy and excited, afraid but feeling powerful, wanting to laugh one minute and cry the next. For many kids, court is yet another experience of feeling vulnerable and intimidated. For others, it is the first time they feel some power.

> Court was definitely a good thing for me. I felt so much better after I heard my uncle admit to what he had done.
> LAUREL, SIXTEEN-YEAR-OLD ABUSED BY UNCLE

You need to decide where you are with all your feelings. This is a decision *you* get to make; no one else can decide for you. When you figure out how you feel and what you feel comfortable doing, you need to speak up and let the adults around you know. That means telling your family, the state's attorney (prosecutor), the social workers, and the police how you feel about testifying.

You are the person who needs to have a voice about this and who needs to be heard. If you don't want to testify, say so. If you want to testify but are feeling scared about it, say so. Others can help you feel more comfortable and secure about what will happen in your situation.

### THE PROSECUTOR MAKES THE FINAL DECISION

The ultimate decision about going to court is made by the prosecutor. You may be ready, willing, and able to go to court and testify but the prosecutor does not believe the case can be won. So your case may not get to court.

Keep in mind that in the course of making her decision, the prosecutor will talk to you, to the police investigating the case, to the protective services worker, and to any other witnesses who might have pertinent information about what happened. After all the material is gathered, she will take a long hard look at whether she can prove to the court that the abuse happened. Her decision will not be made lightly.

---

## GOING TO COURT

Okay, the prosecutor has decided she has a case; the detective who investigated the charges is ready to take the stand; the social worker is prepared to testify on your behalf; and you're going to court. Here are some answers to questions you may have about the whole court experience.

### WILL I HAVE TO SEE THE ABUSER?

If you are going to testify, you will most likely not be allowed in the courtroom until it's time for your testimony. You will be *sequestered*. This means that you will be somewhere other than the courtroom; possibly you will wait in the prosecutor's office, which is usually close to or in the courthouse. You can have a friend or family member be with you. You can play cards, read, talk, or sit quietly while you wait. The whole reason for keeping you out of the courtroom until it's your turn to talk is to prevent you from being influenced by the testimony of others. This way, the prosecutor can make the point that your story is your own and you haven't been coached or swayed by anyone else's version of the story.

If you are going to testify, you will have to enter the courtroom at some point. You will probably have to walk past the abuser to get to the witness stand. Take a look at the sample diagram of the court room (Figure 7.1). Notice where the abuser will be sitting and where the witness stand is. It's really not that far. You can make it.

You have already lived through the worst: the abuse. I know you can live through seeing the abuser in court.

You will enter from the rear of the courtroom. The abuser's back will be toward you, but be prepared for the chance that he or she might turn around to look at you as you enter the courtroom. You do not need to look at him. Focus on someone else in the courtroom or on the person who is escorting you to the front.

During your testimony, you may be asked to identify the person who abused you. At that time, you'll have to look at the abuser. You will be asked something like, "Will you please identify the defendant?" or "Will you please identify the person who abused you?" or, "Is the person who did these things to you sitting in the courtroom?" You may be asked to point at the abuser or to tell where the abuser is sitting in the courtroom. During the rest of your time in the courtroom, you do not have to look at the abuser. You can focus on a family member, your social worker, a friend, or the prosecutor.

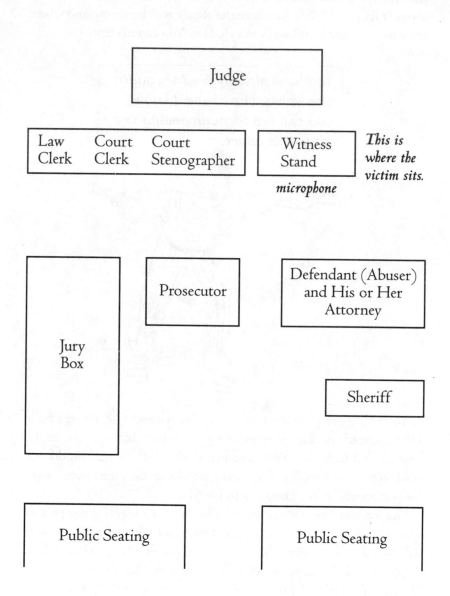

Figure 7.1. Diagram of the courtroom.

Some states have passed laws that permit the use of closed-circuit television for the victim's testimony. This means that the victim never has to enter the courtroom and never has to be face to face with the abuser. The victim is located in another part of the courthouse with a TV camera facing him or her. His or her testimony is sent to the courtroom by way of the TV camera and those in the courtroom watch a big television screen to see and hear the victim's testimony. The victim can also see and hear what is happening in the courtroom via a television set located in the room.

This option is not often used, however. Most of the time this way of testifying is available only to very young victims who would fall apart just by walking into the courtroom or for victims who would be severely traumatized by seeing the abuser face to face. If you want to know whether closed-circuit television is an option for you, be sure to ask the state's attorney who is prosecuting your case.

Some kids don't even consider this an option because they are looking forward to telling the world what the abuser did and seeing his or her response as the truth unfolds. As always, there's no right or wrong way to feel about the whole thing.

## WHAT WILL HAPPEN WHEN I TESTIFY?

When it's your turn to testify, you will be called to the courtroom. You will immediately go up to the witness stand. There you will be asked if you promise to tell the truth about what happened. Many courts use the language, "Do you swear to tell the truth, the whole truth and nothing but the truth?" Other courts may use different language. They all want you to tell the truth—so do it.

After you promise to tell the truth, the *prosecutor* will ask you questions that will help you tell about the abuse. She may have already asked you many of these questions in her office, sometime before the trial—sort of like a practice session. This is perfectly normal procedure. If someone in the courtroom asks you whether you have discussed the case with anyone, like the prosecutor, you should answer honestly and say yes.

After the prosecutor has a chance to ask you questions, the abuser's attorney, the *defense lawyer*, will ask you some questions. This is where it may get tough, so hang in there. Defense attorneys differ greatly, just like every other adult you know. Some have a gentle way about them. Some ask questions that sound like they're mad or arguing with you. The important thing to remember is to simply answer all the questions in a straightforward manner. Tell the truth about what happened to you. Don't argue. Don't make things up if you can't remember a specific incident. Simply say, "I don't remember."

Sometimes a question can be confusing and you might not be sure what the lawyer means. If this happens, just let him know you don't understand the question. It will be up to him to rephrase it in a way that you can understand.

Above all else, tell the truth. Maybe there's a piece of the truth that you think makes you look bad. Don't let that keep you from telling the truth about what happened.

For example, if you are asked, "Why didn't you make the abuse stop" or "Why didn't you tell," say why. Maybe you were afraid of the abuser if you told; maybe you thought no one would believe you; maybe you liked some of the attention and figured putting up with the abuse was the only way to get it. Maybe you were just too darned confused to even think about a way to get the abuse to stop. Whatever you were thinking or feeling, say it—as long as it's the truth.

## HOW DO I HOLD IT TOGETHER ON THE STAND?

If you wonder how you will keep from falling apart, that's simple. Don't worry about holding it together. Crying is a natural response to being hurt and scared. You will be asked to remember some painful memories, and crying is a normal response. Adults often cry on the stand, both men and women.

If you really feel upset, you can turn to the judge and ask for a break so you can collect yourself, or the prosecutor can ask for you. (A break in the court proceedings is called a *recess*.)

If you're feeling angry about the abuse, say so. If you're nervous about being on

> **While you are on the stand:**
> • *Don't lie*
> • *Don't argue*
> • *Don't swear*
>
> • *Do tell the truth*
> • *Do be yourself*
> • *Do ask for a recess if you need to take a break*
> • *Do hang in there*

the witness stand, say so. If you are afraid because you have to see the abuser in the courtroom, say so. Say what you are feeling and *be yourself.*

One word of caution: don't argue or get into a shouting match. You want people to believe what you are saying. Swearing or yelling at the attorneys, the judge, or the abuser is not going to help people believe that you are a credible individual. Express your true emotions. No one expects you to be a robot. You need to verbalize your true emotions just as much as you need to verbalize the true facts. Just do it in the most civil and calm way you can manage.

### WHAT SHOULD I WEAR?

The main thing to remember is that you want people to believe what you have to say. Unfortunately, people often make snap judgments about us based on how we look. Therefore, if you get on the stand dressed in black leather, a safety pin through your earlobe, and a neon green mohawk, you are not going to make a great first impression.

So give some serious thought to how you dress on the day of the trial. The more conservative you seem, the better. Your attorney may make some suggestions about what to wear. If you're used to jeans with holes in them, don't be put off if she suggests a coat and tie or a dress. She's only trying to help you present yourself in the best light.

Remember: First impressions are important.

### WHAT DOES THE COURTROOM LOOK LIKE?

Basically, a courtroom is a big room that can seem intimidating. If you are going to testify, the prosecutor will most likely arrange for you to take a tour of the courtroom some time before the trial so you can get the feel of things. See Figure 7.1 to get an idea of the courtroom layout.

The judge sits up on a platform at the head of the room, behind a table that is called a *bench,* which looks out over the whole courtroom. The *witness stand* is off to the side and in front of the judge's bench.

The witness stand also looks out over the courtroom. This is where each person testifying in the case will sit while she is telling her story.

Next to the witness stand is a long table where several "helpers" sit. These helpers are the *court stenographer* who records everything that takes place in the courtroom, the *court clerk* who marks exhibits and takes an account of any decisions made; a *law clerk* who helps the judge if he or she needs copies of statutes (decisions made in other cases similar to yours) or other legal documents. Like the judge's bench and the witness stand, this table also faces the rest of the courtroom.

The *defense table* faces the judge's bench and is located in front of the witness stand. This is where the abuser sits. He is known as the *defendant*. His lawyer sits there also. He is known as the *defense attorney*. Sometimes there will be other people at the defense table. These may be secretaries or other lawyers who work for the defense attorney.

The attorney you are working with, the *prosecutor*, also sits at a table facing the judge's bench. It is located next to the *jury box* because the prosecutor's job is to convince the jury that the defendant is guilty. The prosecutor works for the state or district where the abuse took place. That's why prosecutors are also known as *state's attorneys* or *district attorneys* (D.A.s).

All trials held in a courtroom are open to the public as well as the press. Therefore, the rest of the seats in the courtroom could be filled by people from the local newspapers as well as some people from your community. Each state varies as to whether or not television cameras are allowed in the courtroom. Most news agencies have an unwritten policy of not publicizing a victim's name.

Try not to let it upset you if you see some familiar faces of neighbors or other people who live in your town. They may be there as a sign of support for you and not just from idle curiosity. Probably, most of the seats in the courtroom will be empty or occupied by law students learning about courtroom procedure, victim assistance advocates, or people waiting their turn for other court cases that are going to be heard that day.

For security, a *sheriff* is located in the courtroom and he sits behind the defendant and in front of the public seating.

If you are not testifying in the case but want to listen to the trial, you'll sit somewhere in the public seating. Some victims find this helpful; they want to see and hear everything that happens and don't mind if people in the courtroom know who they are. Other kids don't want to know anything about the trial and just want someone to tell them when it's all over. Some kids don't know what to think or do until they get to court. Whatever you're feeling is normal and okay. You may even find that your feelings are all mixed up: you may want to go to court, then get there and hate it.

> They read off every detail of what my teacher did to me. It was so embarrassing. There was some old woman behind me and she was crying and patting me and saying, "Oh, you poor thing." I wanted to backhand her.
> CHARLENE, SIXTEEN-YEAR-OLD ABUSED BY ENGLISH TEACHER

You may decide not to go to court, then wish you had. If you can, be somewhere near the courthouse on the day of the trial; then you can make up your mind as the day progresses: Don't go to court initially; then, as you feel stronger, go later. Or go to court in the morning and hate it, then leave and go somewhere safe. It will take some planning on your part to have this as an option, but with the help of some of the adults in your life, you may be able to work it out.

Keep in mind that if you *have* to testify, it's a totally different story. If you are testifying, you *must* go to court and you *must* be available when you are needed to testify.

## WILL THERE BE A JURY?

Whether to have a jury is another issue that varies from state to state. Some states leave this decision up to the defendant (the abuser) and he and his lawyer will decide if a jury trial is in his best interest. In other states, a jury is automatically used for sexual abuse cases. The decision is really not in the hands of the prosecutor.

If you will have to testify, be sure to ask the prosecutor if a jury will be hearing the trial. It is perfectly reasonable to want to know this and to prepare yourself mentally for it. You don't have to do anything special while you are testifying just because a jury will be present. In fact, it may be more helpful to try to block them out of your mind while you're on the stand.

If you're nervous about having a jury present, talk to the prosecutor or your social worker about it. They may be helpful in calming your nerves and giving you tips on how to deal with the jury.

## COURT CAN BE DIFFICULT

I'm not going to kid you; going to court can be a very hard thing to do. The whole idea of having to go into a public place and say what happened may be more than you can handle. The potential embarrassment and worry about what people will think may be causing you to wonder if it's such a hot idea to go through with testifying. These are normal feelings. Most kids who go to court think about these things.

And there are plenty of horror stories out there about how things went wrong in court—how the victim wasn't believed or the abuser got off scot free. For some kids, court is a very negative experience.

Sometimes things do go wrong: reports are misplaced, dates are mixed up, witnesses don't show. As one assistant state's attorney put it, "No matter how good a case we think we have, there's always something that happens that makes me just want to bang my head against the wall."

But, and this is a big but, if the case can be prosecuted and your testimony is vital to winning the case, you've got to make a decision: can I live with a day or two of embarrassment and tension or would I rather spend the rest of my life knowing that I could have done something to stop this abuser and I didn't?

### MAKING A TOUGH DECISION

Keep in mind there are no guarantees that if you go to court and testify, the abuser will be put in jail. There's no guarantee that the abuser will even be found guilty. But (another big but) if you don't try, you will never know whether you could have made a difference.

I don't say this lightly. Court can be a devastating experience for some kids—especially if the abuser is believed and the victim is not. There are some lousy attorneys out there who through their ineptitude and mistakes can lose a case for a victim. However, you need to keep in mind that the courts are still the only system we have to deal with sexual abusers and while it's not perfect, it often does work.

> *Deciding to testify is a very hard decision. Ultimately you have to do what is best for you.*

## PEOPLE WHO CAN HELP

Some states have victim assistance agencies. These folks will personally help you through the whole court process. They'll stay with you if you are sequestered during the trial. They'll sit in the courtroom while you testify so you can have a friendly face to look at. They'll help you write down your Victim Impact Statement. They'll do whatever is in their power to make court a less intimidating and frightening experience for you.

## DO WHAT'S BEST FOR YOU

Going to court is a tough decision. You've got a lot of things to consider. Please, if your case can be prosecuted, think long and hard before you say you won't testify or that you've changed your mind and the abuse never happened. As we've mentioned before, abusers don't usually abuse just one child. All kids who have contact with the abuser are at risk. Maybe it will help you to move forward with testifying if you think about other kids who may have to go through the same horror you have gone through, because nobody would take a stand and say, "Enough!"

*- Take care of yourself!*

Remember: you were not responsible for the abuse and you are not responsible for the abuser's actions, emotions, words. You are responsible for one person: yourself. Be sure you take good care of that person.

However—pay attention now, this is important—do not testify if it is going to undo you. You must take care of you. And no matter how important your testimony may be to the case, you and your mental health are even more important. What is in your best interest? Don't let anyone lay a guilt trip on you or make you feel that you are somehow responsible for the outcome of the trial.

## SENTENCING

The verdict is in; the defendant is guilty. Now, the question is, what consequence will the abuser pay for what he or she has done to you?

Several factors go into a judge's decision in sentencing an abuser. Sometimes a judge may ask that a therapist or psychiatrist evaluate the abuser to see whether he understands that what he did was wrong, to determine whether the abuser would benefit from therapy, and to assess the risk the abuser poses to the community and to other children.

The professional who does the evaluation will then send a written assessment to the judge and make some recommendations about treatment for the abuser. Once the judge gets this report, she will decide what the sentence will be. Here are some options she might consider.

### PROBATION AND COURT-ORDERED THERAPY

Abusers who confess to abusing a child, show that they are sorry for what they have done, and have not been verbally or physically violent to the victim often receive *probation* and *court-ordered therapy*. Being on probation means that an offender must report to a *probation officer* on a regular basis. If he goes out of town, he must let his probation officer know; if he wants to move, he has to tell the probation officer. The system is designed to track the offender and always know where he is. In some states, probation can only last for five years.

Another piece of an abuser's probation may be a *restraining order*. This means that the abuser must keep away from the victim for a specified amount of time.

A judge may also require the abuser to undergo alcohol and drug treatment that includes regular blood tests to make sure the abuser is staying drug free.

*Court-ordered therapy* requires the abuser to go to counseling on a regular basis to deal with the knowledge that he is a sexual offender and to work on making changes in his life. This treatment is usually done with a therapist who has experience dealing with sex offenders and who will work with the other professionals involved in the case like the offender's probation officer, the social worker assigned to the family, and any other therapists who are assisting members of the family.

One goal of court-ordered therapy is to make sure that it really happens. If the abuser misses a counseling session, his probation officer will usually be notified by the therapist and the abuser will get a warning. If an abuser misses several sessions, he might have to go back to court and face the judge to explain his absences. Sometimes abusers who miss too many counseling sessions end up in jail.

## PRISON

Offenders who have abused many victims, who show little remorse for what they've done, or who have been violent and threatening to their victims are often sent to prison. The amount of time an offender will serve varies from state to state as well as case to case. The main thing to remember is that the decision to put an offender in prison is made by the judge or the jury. It has little, if anything, to do with you and your testimony. It's really outside your control.

You may feel very strongly one way or the other about whether the offender goes to prison. For some kids, the idea of a close relative in the "clink" is very embarrassing and something they want to avoid at all costs. For other kids, having the offender go to prison is the only way they will feel validated, believed. They're not worried about what people will think; they want to see justice done and, to them, having the abuser go to prison looks like justice.

You may have an opportunity to give input into the sentencing through the victim impact statement (more about this later), but the decision about jail is not a result of anything you did or didn't do. Ultimately, it is a decision for the judge to make.

## SPECIALIZED TREATMENT

Some offenders need specialized treatment. They have little or no impulse control and have abused dozens of kids. These offenders need special kinds of treatment, which may even include medication to help them curb their sexual impulses. Medical treatment is always done in conjunction with some form of therapy (group or individual). This method of treating sex offenders has been fairly successful over the past ten years or so. However, it is a very specialized treatment and is, therefore, expensive and not available everywhere. It may or may not be an option for the person who abused you.

In deciding on a sentence, the judge will also look at the offender's history, his willingness to seek help, whether he poses a risk to the community, the type of sexual abuse that happened, and the length of time it occurred. There is no usual sentence. Each offender is different and has different treatment needs. Every case is different and there is no guarantee of how the person who abused you will be sentenced. An abuser who is found guilty can be sent to prison, ordered into treatment, given medication, told to stay away from the victim, required to pay for the victim's counseling, or any combination of these.

## PROBATION BEFORE JUDGMENT (PBJ)

PBJ is not an abbreviation for peanut butter and jelly but rather a type of sentencing that some abusers receive—probation before judgment. It is a sentence that can be requested by offenders who are found guilty.

In probation before judgment, the defendant (abuser) is placed on probation for a period of time decided by the court. Many offenders who admit they are guilty of abuse try to get this kind of sentencing because their record will never show a conviction. This means that even though the abuser has admitted committing a crime, it will not be on his record. If the offender successfully completes probation, he will never have to admit on public record or on job applications that he committed a crime because there will be no record of anything.

There is a catch, however; the abuser must *successfully* complete his probation. This may mean being in therapy, receiving drug or alcohol counseling, being monitored for alcohol and drug use, staying away from the victim, and generally staying out of trouble. Failure to do any of these things can take an abuser right off probation and right into prison where he can kiss his PBJ good-bye.

So, while a PBJ may seem to you to let the abuser off too easily, keep in mind this is not the end of the story. The abuser still has to show that he or she can handle being on probation.

## VICTIM IMPACT STATEMENT

As part of the sentencing process, you may be asked to write a victim impact statement. This is your chance to tell the court how the abuse has affected you and your life. You can make the statement in person and speak directly to the judge or, if it's more comfortable, you can write it down and have someone else read it in court. Either way, be sure it's written down in some form. If you decide that you want to make your statement in court, use notes. You may forget a lot of stuff if you get nervous or your knees begin to shake.

# WHEN COURT GOES WRONG

> You can rape a woman on the street and get eight years [in jail]. You can rape your own daughter repeatedly for six years and get three years supervised probation. That's ridiculous!
>
> SOCIAL WORKER FROM DEPARTMENT OF SOCIAL SERVICES

Sometimes the system breaks down and court goes wrong. Sometimes judges make really bad decisions. Sometimes the offender has a better attorney than the victim does. Sometimes kids testify very well and are very believable, but the offender is not convicted. Sometimes the court's action looks like it's telling victims, "You don't matter. What happened was not that big a deal."

If this happens to you, don't give up and don't buy into that message. You *do* matter, what was done to you was *wrong*, and it *is* a big deal. The question is, what can you do about it if the courts don't stand up for you? Who can you find to be your advocate?

## CONVICTION MAY NOT HAVE BEEN POSSIBLE

First, you must remember that if your state tried the case in criminal court, the standards for conviction were very high: beyond a reasonable doubt. This means that you may have done an outstanding job of testifying and presenting yourself on the stand, but the judge or the jury just wasn't convinced beyond that reasonable doubt. Don't beat yourself up about this! You did the best you could do and the result is more of a comment on the judge's or jury's ignorance of the issue of sexual abuse than it is a comment on your performance in the courtroom.

Second, if the offender was not convicted, you may still be in danger, especially if you have to live with her or if she has easy access to you. Ask your social worker or the prosecutor what they are going to do to keep you safe. They may be very limited in actions they can take, depending on your state's laws. But, you should still ask.

> *Remember: If things go wrong in court, it is not a reflection on you. Did you make the best decision for you? If you testified, did you do the best you could do? Then do not spend one minute beating yourself up. Doing your best is all that you can do. Now it's time to move on.*

## HOW YOUR SOCIAL WORKER CAN HELP

One of the things your social worker may be able to do is obtain a Child in Need of Assistance (CINA) petition. This is a petition the social worker presents to the *juvenile court* for a hearing. (Some states call it *family court* rather than juvenile court.) The social worker will try to show that you need protection from the offender and the court needs to step in and help you receive that protection.

Juvenile court is much less formal than criminal court. Remember that in criminal court a case must be proven "beyond a reasonable doubt." But in juvenile court, there is a much less strict standard used and "reasonable cause" is usually enough to show a judge that you are in need of some assistance in being kept safe.

The whole purpose of juvenile court is to protect children. The judge in the juvenile court can find a safe place for you to live; they can order your parents to get counseling or even go to parenting classes so they can be better parents—whatever is needed to see that you are kept safe.

## TAKING CARE OF YOURSELF

Beyond that, there may be little else that others can do for you. You may find that you have to be responsible for protecting yourself and keeping yourself sane. Yes, we're back to that old familiar song: take care of yourself.

The first step in accomplishing this is to believe in yourself: believe that you did the right thing by telling, by testifying, by saying what was true. Believing in yourself also has to do with not accepting the idea that you're not important, that you're a liar, or that the abuse was not that big a deal. There may be a lot of people in your life right now who are telling you these things—don't listen.

The second step in taking care of yourself may be to find a good therapist (see Chapter Eight for more on Helpers). Ask your social worker if he can recommend someone. If medical insurance is not available to cover the cost, then ask if some reduced type of payment can be worked out or if you are eligible for therapy under the Victims of Crime Act (more on this option on page 127). Don't allow the details of life to prevent you from seeking wholeness.

Another part of taking care of yourself may be finding a safe place to live. If your living situation keeps you accessible to the abuser, then speak up and ask your social worker what she can do to find you another living situation. If you have a good friend or relative who would take you in, let the social worker know this so she will have options.

## JUSTICE DOESN'T ALWAYS HAPPEN

You must remember that court proceedings are not always a measurement of the truth, and justice is not always accomplished. You may have learned this firsthand because court did not help to protect you, or actually victimized you again. Nevertheless, you need to remember that you have value, that you have worth, and that you are important. It may be up to you to protect that value and worth; it may be necessary for you to defend your importance, but you can do it. It won't be easy if you're doing it alone. Try to find others to help you. Use your social worker, teachers, guidance counselors, a supportive relative, or friends. Don't isolate yourself just because things went wrong in court. Talk to people; let them know what's happening in your life. Tell again and again and again until someone listens and makes you safe.

Whatever you do, don't give up. You and your life are too precious to lose.

# FORWARD MOTION

# 8

## Healing Is a Choice

*I just wish it would all go away. I'm tired and I don't want to deal with this anymore.*
KATE, SEVENTEEN-YEAR-OLD ABUSED BY GRANDFATHER

THE MAIN THING every one of us who has been sexually abused must decide is this: "Do I want to heal or not?" This may seem like a silly question. But when we look at what it takes to heal, some people decide, "No thanks, I'd rather be a victim for the rest of my life." Others believe staying a victim is their only option. Well, it's certainly an option, but it's definitely not the only one out there and it isn't necessarily the healthiest.

### MAKING THE CHOICE

Healing and becoming a survivor is a conscious choice. It is choosing life and all that your life was meant to be. It is making the decision that you will no longer be a victim of anyone or anything. It is coming to grips with the fact that somebody wronged you. They robbed you of things you had a right to own—like your self-respect, your self-worth, your self-esteem. They robbed you of your self.

Being a survivor is the only healthy option for someone who has been sexually abused. Any other option, like suicide, running away, drugs, or prostitution, is just letting the abuser win, just buying into what the abuser thinks of you.

## HEALING CAN'T HAPPEN IF THE ABUSE IS STILL GOING ON

If you are currently being abused, the decision to heal may be a more difficult one for you to make because you will first have to find a way to make the abuse stop—something you may have been trying to do for years without success. (See Chapter 3 for more on how to stop the abuse and get safe.)

On the other hand, if the abuse has stopped, you may believe that you don't have a decision to make at all, that you are going to be just fine now.

Who are you kidding?

The effects of sexual abuse don't fade into the sunset once the abuse has ended. You don't stop hurting just because the abuse has stopped. What was done to you can work on you the rest of your life unless you spend some time sorting it out, assessing the damage, and making the necessary repairs.

## HEALING TAKES TIME

Becoming a survivor of incest and sexual abuse is not something that happens overnight. It's a process with a lot of steps. Unfortunately, it's not like a recipe or a football play: do these seven things and you get the desired result—a cake or a touchdown.

Healing is more about taking three giant steps forward and eleven baby steps backward. It is doing things over and over, like reminding yourself that you weren't responsible for the abuse. Sometimes you forget what you've learned and have to relearn it. Sometimes you have to work on the same issue again and again during the course of your healing. This can be discouraging. But remember, you're not slow or stupid; this is normal stuff.

## HEALING HAPPENS ON YOUR TIMETABLE

Healing looks different for every person who does it. What may be a hard issue for you to deal with may be a breeze for someone else. And you may sail right through an issue that knocks another person down. There is no timetable and no real order. It isn't like you have to do $x$ $y$ $z$ by a certain time or that you have to accomplish $a$ and $b$ before you can move on to $c$.

Some people decide to be survivors a couple of months after they realize that they were not responsible for the abuse. Others make that choice years later. There is no formula for healing. You do it at your own pace, in your own time, in your own way. The most important thing is to *do it*.

## YOU'RE THE ONLY ONE WHO CAN MAKE THE CHOICE

Your social worker can't make the decision to heal for you. Your friends can't make the decision for you—you've got to do it for yourself. However, you don't have to do it alone. In fact, I'm not sure that it can be done alone. There are lots of therapists, psychiatrists, shrinks, head-doctors (whatever you want to call them) who are working with people like you and me: with people who didn't deserve what happened to them and who are trying to pick up and move on. I strongly recommend therapy for anyone who's been sexually abused.

Healing is a choice.

## THERAPY IS A GOOD PLACE TO START YOUR HEALING

*When my mother first told me she thought I needed some counseling, I just looked at her and said, but I'm not the one who's sick.*
LYNN, SEVENTEEN-YEAR-OLD ABUSED BY BIOLOGICAL FATHER

Many teens feel that therapy is not for them. Like Lynn, you may believe that only "sick" people need therapy. You may feel that you can handle the aftershock of the abuse on your own, that you are invincible and you can get through anything by yourself, even the trauma of abuse.

Some survivors believe the best thing to do is forget about the abuse and get on with their lives. Many of your relatives and friends may believe the same thing and encourage you to do just that. This advice isn't unusual or a sign of stupidity. It means that many people think forgetting is a better choice than dealing with the pain—because there *is* a lot of pain in healing from sexual abuse, and not just for the victims. It can be painful for their families as well.

But *not* dealing with the pain does not get rid of it. Not dealing with it simply puts it on hold. Sooner or later you will have to get back to it because it won't go away by itself. I know this for a fact. I tried to live without dealing with the pain and almost ended up not living. So pay attention here! We need to talk about how therapy can help.

## WHAT THERAPY CAN DO FOR YOU

We have some weird ideas in this society about therapy and mental health. A lot of people think that if you go to therapy you have to be either wealthy or nuts. Or that you have to be hypnotized. Or that you have to lie on a couch and talk to a person who never says more than, "Um-hm." Or, that you'll be pumped full of truth serum and won't have any control over what you say.

Well, these things are just not so. Therapy has come a long way in the last twenty-five years, and you can benefit from that. A lot of very sane, middle-income people see therapists every day of the week. So if you think that therapy is not for you, give it another thought. Therapy is often a real lifesaver for kids who have been sexually abused.

Therapy means dealing with your feelings and the impact sexual abuse has had on your life. This process is a very individual thing and can be different for each person. It is a very healthy place to deal with the issues discussed in Chapter Nine as well as any other concerns you may have.

Therapy is most helpful when you get into it as soon as possible, when your feelings are still out in the open. People who wait too long may find that therapy is more difficult for them because they've forgotten their memories of the abuse, they are unable to get in touch with their feelings about the abuse, or they've shut down emotionally and are afraid to open up to anyone about what happened. If you get into therapy right away, you'll have a better chance of recalling the abuse and the feelings you have experienced.

No one knows exactly how or why therapy works, but the reason seems to be because it gets things out in the open. The process of opening up and sharing your feelings is often a necessary part of the healing process. It's like having a very deep cut that is infected and must be opened up, drained, and exposed to the air so that it can heal.

## YOU HAVE MANY CHOICES OF TYPES OF THERAPY

Over the past twenty years, a lot of progress has been made in dealing with people who have been sexually abused. Many therapists have dedicated their careers to helping victims of sexual abuse. As more has been learned about how people heal from sexual abuse, more options have been made available for treatment. Therefore, you have kind of a smorgasbord to choose from for the type of therapy that will work best for you. Let's look at the options.

### Therapy With A Group

One of the most helpful types for teens who have been sexually abused is *group therapy*. It's easy to believe that you are totally alone, the only kid in the whole world who has experienced this horror. Group therapy helps you to get over the feelings of being alone and different. By meeting with kids who have experienced similar things you begin to see that you're not abnormal, you're not a freak, and you're not alone.

Groups can also offer a lot of support. There may be some things that you find difficult to talk about. Most likely you will find someone in the group talking about the very thing you couldn't. There may be some things that you feel ashamed to discuss with anyone else, but in the group it may just come up as a topic that everyone wants to discuss. Groups can surprise you with their honesty, friendship, and encouragement.

When you look for a group for yourself, remember that the experiences of the other kids in the group should be as similar to yours as possible. In other words, if you were abused by someone in your family, try to find a group with kids who were abused by family members. If you were abused by someone outside the family, try to find a group with kids who were abused by people outside their family.

If there is only time or money in your life for one kind of therapy, try to find a group. It can be a real help in getting started on the journey of your healing.

### Therapy with Just You and a Therapist

*Individual therapy* can be very helpful either in combination with group therapy or by itself. This type of therapy gives you an opportunity to focus in depth on issues or feelings that have been bothering you. While group therapy can be helpful in bringing issues to the surface and making you aware of them, there isn't always a lot of time to really explore your personal issues. Remember, you are sharing group time with six or eight other teens. Sometimes having your very own therapist, who spends one hour a week with just you, can be very beneficial.

If you were abused by a close family member such as your father or sister or someone else living in your home, chances are you and the abuser will need some time apart. However, after acknowledging the abuse and beginning to work on the issues, many families decide they want to get back together. For this reunion to be successful, other types of therapy may be necessary.

## Therapy with the Abuser

Whether the goal is for you and the abuser to live together again or not, it's very often helpful for the victim's angry feelings and the abuser's feelings of remorse to be shared. Before this can happen, though, the abuser must take responsibility for what he did. This may come about through the abuser's participation in group therapy or individual therapy. Like victims, abusers also benefit from group therapy. Obviously, the abuser would be in a group with other offenders. For more information on offender therapy, see Chapter Thirteen, What You Should Know About Offenders.

Once the abuser has acknowledged his responsibility, it may be appropriate for the abuser and the victim to meet. This meeting would take place with the abuser's therapist and the victim's therapist present. The abuser could then tell the victim that he acknowledges full responsibility for what happened and state any feelings of regret or sorrow that he may have.

This meeting, which is often called a responsibility session, can also serve as an opportunity for the victim to express anger and hurt directly to the abuser. The victim may also want to ask questions or state some concerns. For more on *responsibility sessions,* see page 220.

A meeting like this should take place in a safe and neutral setting, like a therapist's office. Decisions about future meetings and reestablishing contact between the victim and the abuser can also be discussed. It's important to have input from the therapists so that things move along at a pace that is comfortable for you and so that you are not put at risk for being re-abused.

## Therapy with the Nonoffending Parent

Another relationship that often needs help in healing is the relationship between the victim and the parent who did not abuse but who you thought should have protected you from the abuse. Most often this is the mother.

Many teens have a lot of anger toward this parent for different reasons. Some parents didn't believe the teen when he revealed the abuse. Some parents blamed the victim for what happened. Some parents were constantly jealous of the relationship the victim had with the abuser and felt left out. Some parents pushed the teen toward the abuser to avoid having to be involved themselves.

Many kids feel angry because they simply believe that their parent should have known what was going on. Whatever your reasons for your anger, they need to be aired and dealt with. Both you and your nonoffending parent (or the person you think should have protected you) need to be honest about your feelings and "own" them. You will also need to listen to one another and hear each other's point of view. By doing this, a new, more honest relationship can develop. This kind of healing can best take place when a therapist is there to guide the process.

### Therapy with the Family

Once family members deal with their individual feelings and issues, they are ready to start working on relationship issues within the family. They are ready for *family therapy*. Family therapy recognizes the importance of each family member in the family system. This includes brothers and sisters and any other significant household members. It's

You have many choices of types of therapy.

important to keep in mind that incest or sexual abuse is always a *family* problem, not just the victim's, not just the abuser's. And every member of the family is affected when abuse is revealed.

Family reunification can be a very slow process. It can start out with contact among family members occurring only in the safety of a therapist's office. As progress is made, contact can be lengthened to include a meal and eventually an overnight visit.

Every step should be looked at and discussed with a therapist and each family member should be allowed to say how he or she feels about the proposed contact. If a therapist senses any reluctance to have contact or to increase the contact, this reluctance should be thoroughly explored before proceeding.

### THERAPY OVERLOAD

You may be sitting there saying, "Oh good. I can give up my life and just do therapy. Are you sure you didn't miss someone else I could have therapy with?"

Okay, okay. I know that therapy alone can seem overwhelming, especially if you're involved in many different types. I also know that you can get to a point where you really resent the time and money and effort you're putting into healing. Sometimes it is a good idea to take a "vacation" from therapy. But you can't take a vacation until you begin the work.

There's no magic about therapy. It is slow, often painful, work. It takes patience and courage and desire. Even if there is no hope that your family will be reunited, do yourself a favor and get into a group or individual therapy or both. Do it for yourself. Do it because you're worth it. Do it so that you can have the future you deserve. Like the commercial says, Just Do It.

## WHICH THERAPIST IS FOR ME?

After all that has happened, you might question the value of turning to an adult for help, especially if the person who abused you was an adult. I totally understand. You may have good reason to doubt the trustworthiness of adults and may feel that the last thing you want to do is talk to or lean on one for advice or assistance.

Unfortunately, there aren't any teenage therapists out there—at least none that I know of. So you're going to have to take the plunge and take a chance on trusting an adult.

There are all kinds of therapists with many different professional backgrounds. Some are trained as psychiatrists, others as psychologists, social workers, or pastoral counselors. You may know them as shrinks, head shrinkers, talking friends, or worry doctors.

The most important thing is to find one who is right for you. Begin by talking to your social worker or child protection services worker, calling a mental health hot line in your area, or using a community information and referral service. You want to find someone who is licensed in the counseling or psychiatric field as well as having specialized training and experience working with sexual abuse victims and their families.

Here are some other things you will want to look for in a therapist:

*Do you feel comfortable with the therapist?* This may seem an obvious thing to consider, but if you've spent a large part of your life being denied the right to say, "No, I don't like this," you may need a reminder that you are the one who gets to decide whether this is the therapist for you. Now, let me hasten to add that this decision is going to take a couple of sessions. You can't just walk in and say, "Wup, no, she's a blonde and all blondes are bimbos. I'm not staying." Or, "Yuk, look at that tie. I couldn't possibly sit in the same room with someone with such bad taste." You've got to give it some time—at least three or four sessions.

> **You get to decide if you feel comfortable with the therapist. Be fair, though. Getting comfortable can take a little time—definitely more than one or two sessions.**

*Do you feel judged by the therapist?* A good therapist will not judge you in any way and will not "tell" you how to do things or instruct you. A good therapist will listen to you and try to understand your feelings and thoughts and help guide you through the healing process. Your therapist is your guide, not your conscience. He or she should be familiar enough with the healing process to know when the roadblocks are going to come and how to help you get around them.

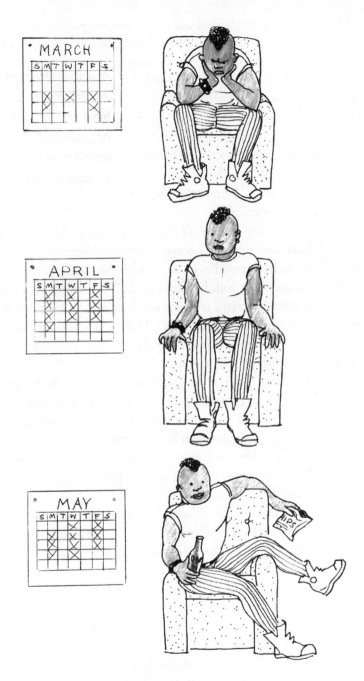

Getting comfortable with therapy takes time.

*Does the therapist try to control you? Should* is not a word in a good therapist's vocabulary. His job is to help you get back your sense of power
and control, not to tell you step by step
what to do. This may not be as wonderful as it sounds. You may feel so beat up
that you would just love for someone to
walk into your life, organize it, and tell
you how to carry on. Your therapist
won't be insensitive to that, but instead
of taking over he will help you figure out
how to manage your life.

> *A good therapist
> will help you learn
> how to take charge
> of yourself. She
> won't try to take
> charge of you.*

*How much money will it cost?* Therapy is not cheap. Most families rely
on their health insurance to cover a substantial part of their therapy
bills. Some therapists will work out a time payment plan while others
have what's known as a sliding scale. This means that you pay a per-
centage of what you earn. If you're working at McDonalds for $4.25
an hour, you may have to pay only $15.00 per session. It varies from
therapist to therapist. But asking about payment is a reasonable
request of any prospective therapist.

Sometimes courts will order the abuser to pay for the victim's therapy. If the abuser was tried in criminal court, you and your family can
ask the prosecuting attorney (the state's attorney) to make payment of
therapy part of a plea agreement or court order at the time of sentencing. Not only can this save you the expense of paying for something
that was never your fault, but it can also offer the abuser a way of making partial restitution for the crime.

There are publicly funded agencies that specialize in treating victims. Their services are available at no cost or very little cost. To learn
about them contact your local sexual assault center (you can find the
number in the white pages of the telephone directory under Sexual
Assault Recovery Center, Sexual Assault Hotline, Sexual Assault
Resource Center, and so on) or your local department of social services (they're usually under government listings in your phone book.
You need to know the county or city you live in and then look up
Social Services under that jurisdiction). Both types of agencies may be
able to offer you services at very little cost.

And then there is VOCA (Victims of Crime Act) a federal law that says any victim of a crime is entitled to receive help. That help can take many forms, but in your case, it could take the form of free therapy.

There is a federal fund, the Victim's of Crime Fund, which is administered under the Victims of Crime Act (VOCA). This fund gives money to each state so the state can provide certain direct services to crime victims.

If you were sexually abused, you are the victim of a crime. If you have decided to get therapy (a very good decision to make) the cost may be covered since therapy is one of the services provided for under VOCA.

> **The Victims of Crime Act (VOCA) is a federal law. Therefore, every state gets some VOCA funds. If a police report has been filed about the abuse, you may be eligible for free psychological services through VOCA.**

Because each state distributes the money as it sees fit, there is no standard format for how you should apply. Each state does it differently, and each state varies in the amount of money available for crime victims. The one common rule is that a police report must have been filed about the abuse in order for you to be eligible for free psychological services. Ask your social worker if she can help you apply. You won't know what's available to you until you ask.

## HOW A DOCTOR CAN HELP

Doctors can be a valuable part of a child sexual abuse investigation team. Like therapists in this field, doctors require special training in assessing the impact of sexual abuse on a victim. The doctor's job is primarily to gather medical evidence of the abuse that will support (or *corroborate*) a victim's statement.

However, examining an adolescent for the purpose of gathering evidence of sexual contact is not always necessary. This is because it is very difficult to tell whether an adolescent has had sexual intercourse. Their bodies have begun to mature and do not always show the effects of intercourse. *The one exception* is a forceful sexual assault from which tearing, bleeding, and possibly internal damage occur. Any forceful sexual assault should be followed immediately by medical attention at a hospital or rape crisis center.

Doctors who are trained in dealing with victims of sexual abuse can also be helpful in giving routine medical examinations. You may want to consider getting a medical exam just so you can be sure that you are free of disease and/or any unseen injury. Knowing this can be reassuring and provide you with a chance to ask questions about your body that may be on your mind. You may have some concerns about what is normal or want some specifics about sexuality and sexual response. Don't ever be afraid to ask questions, especially when it comes to your health.

If you were abused by a male, you may prefer a female doctor or nurse practitioner. Try to find someone with whom you are comfortable. You've had enough of being touched by people who make you nervous or tense. Many public health clinics have doctors and nurses on staff who are trained to deal with adolescents and especially sexually abused adolescents. Here again, your local sexual assault or rape crisis center can be of help in finding a good doctor.

> *Do yourself a favor and consider getting a medical checkup. If you have a sexually transmitted disease, your doctor can prescribe medication to clear it up or at least relieve the symptoms. And if you are HIV positive, you may be able to stay well longer if you know about it and do the things your doctor tells you to do to take care of yourself.*

## TAKING CARE OF YOURSELF

Yes, that's right. I'm singing the same old song: take care of yourself. Don't tune me out now. So I'm not your parental unit; consider me your older sister, your older sister who really cares about what happens to you. I mean it when I tell you that getting into therapy of some sort is the very best gift you could possibly give yourself. That doesn't mean that if you find yourself in a negative therapy situation (the therapist is incompetent, judgmental; the people in your group aren't in the same boat you are) that you should stay with that bad situation. What I do mean is that when you find healthy, helpful therapy, your life is going to change—for the better.

As a frightened seventeen-year-old off to college three weeks after telling my mother about the abuse, I got into some pretty pathetic therapy. Twenty-some years ago, there weren't many professionals out there dealing with incest and sexual abuse. Over the years, I've had pathetic, fair, and lifesaving therapists. My dearest wish is that you will be blessed with a counselor or therapist or social worker who will guide you and encourage you along the road of healing.

Healing is not an easy journey, but it is so worth it! Get into therapy and get under way.

# 9

## Respecting How You Survived

*These kids go out every day and participate in society through school, through church, through family and pretend that things are "normal" and "healthful." The energy these kids use to just function daily is amazing. Everything they've been through and they have maintained this "normal" life. . . All the pain that's inside that they keep hidden from so many people.*

THERAPIST FROM SEXUAL ASSAULT RECOVERY CENTER

**W**HEN YOU ARE BEING SEXUALLY ABUSED, a lot of your time and energy are spent on trying to survive—on coping with the trauma, the horror, the invasion. It's not an easy thing to do. Besides putting your energy into surviving, you also need energy for the other things in your life like brushing your teeth and getting dressed each morning, being a member of your family, going to school, keeping a job, participating in sports or clubs, being involved in your church, or maintaining your friendships. Your life requires more energy than the average teenager's life.

So, first of all, give yourself a pat on the back for working up the stamina to cope with the abuse. You may not feel energetic—you may feel totally exhausted, but you still go on, don't you? You still roll out of bed every day and do the things your life requires. Give yourself another pat on the back.

In fact, keep that arm ready. This whole chapter is about pats on the back—giving yourself credit and respecting yourself for what you've done to survive the abuse. Some of it may not be pretty. In fact, some of it may have been really hurtful to you or to others. But remember: what you did, you did to survive.

## EMOTIONAL COPING TECHNIQUES

There are a lot of coping techniques that are used by everyone who is sexually abused. It doesn't matter whether they are male or female, young or old. All of us have ways to deal with what's happening. Some of these techniques are incredibly creative. Some of them can be very hurtful. In your healing, you'll be able to decide which coping mechanisms to keep and which to throw out.

Here are some of the emotional coping techniques that you may have been using and didn't even know it. You may have thought you were the only one in the world that did this stuff. Not true. All of us use some of them.

### THE "AS SOON AS" COPING TECHNIQUE

Many kids who have been sexually abused use the "as soon as" method of coping. They believe that "as soon as the abuse stops, I'll be fine." "As soon as I get a job and get out of here, everything will be okay." "As soon as I'm in college, everything will be different." "As soon as he stops drinking or she finds a new husband, everything will be back to normal."

But the effects of the abuse won't simply evaporate after you have gotten away from the abusive situation. The feelings you have about yourself won't suddenly disappear when you no longer have to deal with the abuser.

"As soon as" may get you through the day or the month or the year, but it won't necessarily work for the rest of your life. "As soon as" is just another way of avoiding the abuse and the impact it may have had on your life.

The only "as soon as" that works is this: "As soon as I deal with what happened to me, I can start to feel better about myself and get on with my life."

## THE "IT'S NOT THAT BAD" COPING TECHNIQUE

Another way of coping is to tell yourself that it's not that bad. "This is no big deal. Lots of kids have it worse. After all, there are kids who have no place to sleep, no food to eat, no nice clothes to wear—things aren't really that bad."

Wrong. You don't get to go to the bonus round.

Okay, sometimes it does help to minimize situations, to put them in perspective, but this is not one of those times.

Let's face it; all of us have a need to believe in the basic goodness of the people in our lives, especially if they are our parents, family members, or people that we look up to. We need to hold on to the idea that they are decent, loving, trustworthy human beings and we will do almost anything to hang on to that image.

If one of those people is doing something hurtful to you, you may find yourself rationalizing it by saying, "He didn't mean it; he was drunk" or "She just needs some love and affection because my father treats her like dirt." You may keep telling yourself that things could be worse.

This can help you to get through the day-to-day routine. It may help you get out of bed every morning and face the world. But it may also keep you from feeling the anger and rage at what's been done to you. If you're not ready to feel that rage yet, then this coping technique will protect you.

At some point, however, you will have to stop thinking "It's not that bad" and deal with the reality of what happened. Do it when you're ready.

## THE "ONLYS" COPING TECHNIQUE

Another way to keep yourself from facing up to the reality of the situation is to use the onlys: "It was *only* once and he was really sorry." "It was *only* my soccer coach, not my father and that's supposed to be worse." "It was *only* fondling, not rape."

Well, the news is that it *only* takes one time to have the world be different. And if it was *only* your uncle or sister or babysitter or family friend, it has still left a wound on your soul. So don't try to diminish your pain or fear by lying to yourself.

The "onlys" may get you through the worst of it. But there may come a time when you need to throw them aside and stand up and yell, "This stinks." The "onlys" won't be necessary anymore because you will be facing the truth about what happened to you and taking the healing steps necessary to get beyond it.

## THE DENIAL COPING TECHNIQUE

Many people who were sexually abused find that denying it ever happened keeps them sane. They find it's easier to pretend nothing happened than to face up to the knowledge that the people they have a right to trust and be loved by are the people who are hurting them the most. Boys especially may find the denial tactic useful. Many guys believe that a male should never be a victim in the first place. If he becomes one, then he can at least say, "It wasn't really abuse," or "It never happened."

Another form of denial is to say, "Okay, it happened, but I'm fine. It didn't bother me." You can really get to a point where you convince yourself that everything is fine. It's much easier not to think about what happened than to face up to the trauma of it.

All of us have the potential to deny things in our life that make us unhappy or are hurtful. It's nothing to be ashamed of. But there may come a time when you can no longer deny that you were abused or that the abuse had a negative impact. That may be a scary time or a very angry time. You don't have to handle it alone. There are a lot of good therapists out there who help kids who have been sexually abused through the healing process. If denial is necessary to keep you sane right now, okay. But when the time comes to deal with the abuse, don't do it alone. Find a therapist and work it through with his or her help. (For more on finding a therapist, see page 118.)

## THE "FORGETTING" COPING TECHNIQUE

It may seem hard to believe that anybody could forget being sexually abused, but there are many men and women walking around who have totally squashed any memory of their abuse. Forgetting is a very powerful coping mechanism. It allows victims to move on with their lives and never have to deal with the impact the abuse has had on them. Or at least think they're not dealing with it.

Sexual abuse always has an impact whether we are willing to acknowledge it or not. The effects can be seen in the way we interact with other people, the hurtful things we do to our bodies (alcohol, drugs, self-mutilation), and our basic attitude toward life. Forgetting may help victims to get through each day, but at some level, their bodies know what happened. A lot of folks end up with a drinking problem or a marital problem or some other kind of emotional problem without realizing that the root of all these is in their childhood and the abuse they suffered.

Again, forgetting may be necessary for someone to survive. With luck, however, she will remember the abuse and begin the healing. And I really do mean "with luck." How horrible to go through your life with one troubling issue after another and never be able to sort it all out because you can't remember the one thing that's creating all these difficulties. Survivors who have their memories often have an easier time of healing because their issues are on the table.

## THE "SPLITTING" COPING TECHNIQUE

One of the most creative coping techniques is to "split." (The medical term is *dissociation*.) Essentially, this is an "out of body experience." Your body remains in one place but your mind and soul go somewhere else (often to the ceiling) until the abusive event is over. When the abuser leaves, and you are alone, your mind, soul, and body come back together again.

Everyone has the capability of dissociating. Lots of people talk about driving from one place to another and not remembering how they got there. That's a form of dissociation. For people who are abused, dissociation becomes more pronounced. They literally leave their bodies during the abuse and focus their attention elsewhere.

> I was about nine or ten; my father and I were driving in the car. I can't remember what he said to me or did to me but I was definitely not in my body. I mean, my whole visual memory is of the back of his head, the back of my head, the back of the front seat of the car and that's because I was literally on the ceiling at the back of the car. So all I can remember is how things looked from the back seat— but my body was in the front seat!
>
> RICHIE, FIFTEEN-YEAR-OLD ABUSED BY BIOLOGICAL FATHER

Some kids count the flowers or stripes on their wallpaper. Other kids do the multiplication tables. Others just totally numb out. Whatever it is you do, remember that this is something positive; this technique is keeping you from cracking up. It is saving your life.

There is a downside to splitting, however. It can go too far. When a person splits too far, she can't bring her body, soul, and mind back together again and she may develop multiple personalities.

Multiple personality disorder (MPD) is a very unique diagnosis. It is made only after an experienced therapist has determined that a person has truly developed different personalities to cope with the trauma of the abuse and switches unconsciously from personality to personality as a way of avoiding his pain. People with MPD are often not aware of their personalities (alters). Therefore, they often find themselves unable to recall things they said or did the day before because another personality was in control. Before they know they have MPD, many survivors think they are nuts or are surrounded by people who are trying to make them crazy.

> My Mom and I were having a lot of trouble getting along. She kept accusing me of lying because she would say, "You did such and such" and I would deny it because I truly believed I hadn't done it. It turns out it was one of my alters who did it and I legitimately did not remember the event.
>
> KARLA, FIFTEEN-YEAR-OLD ABUSED BY STEPFATHER

MPD is not a diagnosis that can be made quickly or easily. It is also not a diagnosis that is frequently made. Be careful with a therapist who wants to label you with MPD too quickly. For more information on multiple personalities, you may want to read *United We Stand* by Eliana Gil, published by Launch Press (1990).

Splitting can also get in your way when you're trying to establish an intimate relationship. If you blank out every time things get stressful, there isn't much chance to work things through with a friend or marriage partner.

Does this mean that because you sometimes "split" you have MPD? Of course not. Does this mean that you will never manage to have a long-term, loving relationship with someone? No! Just remember that every coping mechanism can have a negative side to it. The trick is to keep the things that are helpful and get rid of the things that are harmful.

## PHYSICAL COPING TECHNIQUES

Beyond the coping you're doing with your mind and emotions, you may also be doing some physical stuff in an effort to get a handle on your pain. I really want you to take a look at these things because the physical stuff can hurt you more terminally than the emotional stuff. It all hurts, but if you're drinking or drugging, driving recklessly, or starving yourself, you are putting your well-being in a whole lot more danger than if you're telling yourself "It's not that bad." So, again, pay attention and let's talk about how you can make some changes.

### EATING DISORDERS

You are probably aware of the terms *anorexia nervosa* and *bulimia*. In case you're not, let me explain.

Anorexia is basically slow starvation. The person does not eat enough food to provide the energy and nutrients the body needs and she literally starves—sometimes to death.

Bulimia, on the other hand, is stuffing yourself and then vomiting. It may sound gross if this isn't your form of self-abuse, but people who have this disorder get tremendous cravings for food. They have to eat—pints of ice cream, whole pizzas, bags of cookies, huge meals—and then they force themselves to throw it all up. Their bodies never get a chance to absorb any of the nutrients that might have been in the food.

Both anorexia and bulimia have to do with control. A person who is being sexually abused often feels she has no control over her life or her body. So she decides that the one thing she *can* control is the food she puts in her mouth and she does that in an extreme way.

Another eating disorder is obesity—plain old fat. Some victims of sexual abuse use food as comfort. There is such tremendous pain inside that they need to do something about it. They find that food brings contentment even if it's only for a short time. Other kids who are sexually abused think that being fat will protect them from the abuser. If they look unattractive, maybe the abuser will leave them alone.

You don't have to suffer from any of these eating disorders. There are therapists and counselors who are specially trained in this field who can help you. Don't make the mistake, though, of seeking out counseling for an eating disorder without also getting counseling for the abuse. The eating problem is a *result* of the abuse. You can't solve one without the other.

## DRUGS AND ALCOHOL

Many teenagers experiment with drugs and alcohol; this is often a symptom of their rebellion or need to break free from Mom and Dad. Many teenagers also end up dying because of this experimentation. Drunk driving is one of the leading killers of teens in this country.

A teenager who has been sexually abused will often skip over the experimenting part and go right to numbness and oblivion. Drugs and alcohol can remove you from your present circumstances, make you feel powerful, help you to forget your pain. They can also kill you.

You may think, "Who cares? I'd be better off dead anyway." I care and I am confident that there are other people in your life who also care. Killing yourself with drugs and alcohol is not the answer to your anger and rage at what somebody else did to you. You're letting the abuser win by allowing his or her perception of you as worthless to become your perception of yourself. Please don't allow that to happen.

If you're ready to kick the habit, then get some help. Call Alcoholics Anonymous or Narcotics Anonymous. You can find them in the white pages of your phone book or, in some cases, in the Yellow Pages under Counseling. You can also ask someone at your school to recommend a local program. Just like eating disorders, however, drug addiction and alcoholism are the end products of abuse. They won't go away or stay away until you also work through the issues of being sexually abused.

## SMOKING

Former United States Surgeon General C. Everett Koop has quoted many recent studies proving that nicotine (a drug found in cigarettes) is as addictive as heroin. In other words, you really do need that cigarette (just like a junkie needs a fix)! Smoking is an extremely difficult habit to kick. Many smokers know the bad news about cigarette smok-

ing: it's the leading cause of lung cancer; it may even cause cancer in those who are around the smoker. But the smokers still persist in their habit. As a former smoker, I think that's because we don't really care. We feel that we are worthless anyway and lung cancer will get us off the planet just that much sooner.

As you begin to heal, however, you may start to feel that you are worth something and that you don't need that cigarette anymore as your reward, your way of keeping others at a distance, your way of looking grown up. Even though our society is making it more difficult to smoke, we still see a smoker as a step above a drug addict or drunk driver—as more socially acceptable. This semi-acceptance adds to the difficulty in kicking the habit. Do it when you are ready; just don't kid yourself that it's not self-abusive.

## SELF-MUTILATION

> I stood at the bus stop and sliced my wrist. I just wanted to see the blood. It was like, Oh, I'm still alive. My sister went nuts.
>
> DEBORAH, FIFTEEN-YEAR-OLD ABUSED BY UNCLE

A lot of kids, boys and girls, inflict pain on themselves. They cut, hit, pinch, burn, scratch, and bite themselves. There are lots of reasons that you may be doing this to yourself.

## I Exist

Often kids who are sexually abused have difficulty feeling. The only way they can survive is to shut down emotionally. If you've turned everything off, you may not be sure you can still feel something. Hurting yourself may be your way of feeling something, even if it's pain. You may figure that if you see blood, you will know you're still alive.

## Rage

Sometimes the anger about what's happening gets so great that you may feel the only thing to do is to be violent, and you become violent with yourself. You may pretend that the pain you're inflicting on your own body is really happening to the abuser. Some kids are so angry at the abuse, the abuser, or the parent who's not protecting them that they feel they need to make a visible statement of their anger by hurting themselves.

> My Mom and I had a fight. She called my grandparents to tell them what a miserable person I am and whined to them about me. I was so mad! I felt like killing myself or something. I slit my wrist with a modeling knife. I wanted to emphasize how much I hated what was happening.
> SUZANNE, FOURTEEN-YEAR-OLD ABUSED BY MOTHER'S BOYFRIEND

## Punishment

You may feel that your body needs to be punished because it has responded to some of the sexual stimulation, or you may still be caught in the responsibility trap and feel that you're bad because you are being abused and therefore need to be punished.

> I just started to slit my wrists. My parents were fighting and I decided it was all my fault and they would be happier without me.
> JOEY, FIFTEEN-YEAR-OLD ABUSED BY STEPFATHER

## Ugliness

You may think that if you can make yourself unattractive, the abuser will stop hurting you and leave you alone. I met a young woman I'll call Nicole, who had beautiful tawny-colored skin, huge eyes a dazzling shade of green, and long hair the color of caramels. She was absolutely gorgeous—from the left side. When she turned to face me fully, I could see a horribly disfiguring scar down the right side of her face. This is how Nicole explains what happened:

> He always told me I was so beautiful that he couldn't help himself. So, when I was fourteen, I took a razor blade and did this. It didn't stop him. . . . and now I have to live with this face for the rest of my life.

### Help

It could be that this is your way of crying out for help. Maybe if somebody sees all the slash marks on your arms or the burn marks on your legs, they'll ask what's going on and then you can get help.

Self-mutilation is another coping mechanism. It's something you may be doing to keep yourself alive. It's also hurting you. You don't deserve the pain the abuser has given you and you don't deserve the pain you're giving yourself.

It is not easy to stop hurting yourself. You may not be able to stop on your own. If you're in therapy, you can make a contract with your therapist that you will not hurt yourself until your next meeting with her. And then make another contract for the next week. If you're not in therapy, it can be harder. You can try making a contract each day with yourself. Tell yourself you will not hurt your body in any way for one full day. And then each morning, make the contract again. If you have a good friend whom you trust, maybe you can make a contract with him each day. Just stop hurting yourself. You don't deserve to be hurt by yourself or anyone else.

> *You were not responsible for the abuse. You do not have to be punished for what happened. Please, please don't hurt yourself anymore.*

## SLEEPING AROUND AND PROSTITUTION

When you think about it, sleeping around is another form of self-abuse: it tells the world you don't really value your body, that you basically treat yourself like trash. Additionally, in this world of numerous sexually transmitted diseases and the epidemic of AIDS, having frequent sex with a number of different partners is like playing Russian Roulette—you never know when you're going to get it—another big, "I don't care about myself" message.

> **LOVE**
> **does not have to hurt,**
> **does not have to cost,**
> **does not have to be sex.**

If you're a girl, you may think that the only way to get attention is to "put out." If you're a guy, you may feel that you need to prove how macho you are by sleeping with anything in skirts. Or no matter whether you're a guy or a girl, you may simply want some love and affection and your experience is that the only way to get it is to be sexual with someone. Not so. You can have nonsexual contact with someone that is loving and affectionate and nurturing. You may need to *learn* how to do that, but since you've made the healthy choice to be in therapy (you have made that healthy choice, haven't you?), your therapist and/or group members can help you.

Then there's prostitution. Studies show that a large majority of prostitutes, both males and females, were sexually abused when they were children.

Prostitution is a whole lot different from sexual abuse. When you were being abused by someone whom you should have been able to trust, you had no power, no control over what happened. Even if you set up circumstances where you knew you would be abused but figured that was necessary to gain what you wanted or needed, you were still the victim; you were still not responsible. Prostitution, on the other hand, is a choice—and not a healthy one.

You may have chosen prostitution because it makes you feel powerful, or because you like the extra money. While you *can* get money from prostitution, you can *also* get babies, abortions, beatings from pimps or johns, jail time, diseases, AIDS, or death. Ultimately, you can end up with nothing left of yourself.

Just like sleeping around, prostitution also sends the message: "I don't care about me, I'm worthless, this means nothing, I am nothing." This kind of thinking lets the abuser win. It validates exactly what the abuser thought of you—you're cheap and unimportant. That's wrong! You are valuable. You are important—and your wants, dreams, and needs are worthy. Don't let the abuse and the abuser take that away from you. (See Chapter 12 for more information on sex and the way it can be.)

## BECOMING A DAREDEVIL

Driving recklessly, taking dares, doing things that could get you in trouble with the police, risking your physical well-being in any way are all tactics you may be using to deal with the abuse. Once again the "I'm worthless" monster rears its head and you may have found all kinds of things that may end your life or, at the very least, cause you to get seriously hurt.

Guys are more likely to use this technique of coping. They're stuck with all the macho junk to begin with. Then add the sexual abuse on top of that and they will literally kill themselves trying to prove just how "manly" they are.

> I kept throwing myself in front of my friends' cars. They would never go really fast or anything. I just wanted to see if it would hurt. . . Actually, I just wanted to see what it would be like to be dead.
> RANDY, THIRTEEN-YEAR-OLD ABUSED BY BIOLOGICAL MOTHER

## BEING PERFECT

You may have decided to cope with being abused by becoming "superkid." You get terrific grades in school, you belong to a lot of clubs, you're everybody's favorite babysitter, and you're super-responsible and mature. You are a chameleon; you can blend in in any situation. From the outside, your life may look wonderful and you probably work very hard at keeping the "pretty picture" of your family intact. You don't act out or do drugs or alcohol. Your favorite sentence is, "Everything's fine."

Some kids believe that there is so much garbage and scum in their lives that they need to do everything possible to remove themselves from it, so they become perfect. They think they need to "be good" so people will like them, so they will have value.

Wrong. Your value and worth do not come from the things you do or say. Value and worth are gifts; you got them when you were born and they are still with you, in spite of what you have been told, taught, or feel about yourself.

Perfectionism can be hard to give up; it becomes a habit, a crutch. It can give you migraine headaches, ulcers, or severe depression. It can also make you a lousy marriage partner, parent, and friend. Wanting to do things well is a good goal. The question is, what's the cost? Your health? Your relationships? Your life?

If you're a perfectionist, do yourself a favor and try to make a little mistake once in a while: don't dot all your "i's" and cross all your "t's" on your next homework assignment. Or do something really well instead of perfectly: brush your teeth for only two minutes instead of your usual five.

You don't *have* to be perfect. You can be who you are with all your humanness and the imperfections that go along with being human. The world will not end, your life will not be over, and the bogey-man will not get you because you make a mistake. *And*, you will still be a valuable and worthy human being.

## SUICIDE

The ultimate attempt to cope with sexual abuse is suicide. Lots of people in this country, both adults and teens, think that suicide is the only way out of their circumstances. When you think about it, though, suicide is not really coping; it's an ending. Listen to this:

Suicide is a permanent
(eternal, forever, unending,
constant) solution to a
temporary problem.

Did you really hear that? Suicide is forever. It isn't like you check out of life for a couple of years, and then step back in when things get better. Or that you get to come to your own funeral and see if the abuser is really sorry for what he or she did to you.

Suicide is permanent, forever. And the problems you're trying to get away from are temporary—only for a little while. You may not feel that way right now. You may feel like there's no way out. But there is; you *can* make the abuse stop: you can tell. (See Chapter Three to learn how to tell.) Suicide is NOT the way to stop the abuse. Suicide is a way to let the abuser win, and that is NOT okay.

If you're feeling suicidal right now:

- Turn to page 68 for some words of encouragement from kids who have lived through sexual abuse.

- Call your local suicide prevention hot line. You'll find it in the phone book Yellow Pages under Counseling or in the Action Index (if your phone book has one) under Suicide.

- Write down all the reasons you have for choosing to live. There may not seem to be many right now, but there are definitely a few, like the people in your life who need you (a younger sibling? a child you babysit? a friend? the kid you tutor on Saturdays?). How about the nice thing that's going to happen next month (a dance, a big date, a job interview, a trip)? Come on. I know there are at least one or two reasons you have to live. If you can't think of any, let me suggest one: plain old hardheadedness and unwillingness to let the abuser win. What about good old-fashioned curiosity about how your life is going to turn out once you get beyond the abuse? Because you *will* get beyond the abuse. You *will* find the life that waits for you beyond sexual abuse and incest.

- Tell a trusted friend about your suicidal feelings. Spend as much time as you can with that friend—don't stay alone. Make an agreement with him or her that you will not hurt yourself for the next twenty-four hours.

- Make that same agreement the next day.

- Turn to page 66 for a list of Blues Busters

Whatever you do, *don't kill yourself.* You were not responsible for what happened; you are not worthless or bad or dirty or whatever other negatives you've been believing about yourself. You are a valuable person who has been told that you are not. The value is still there. You just need to see it for yourself and that's what this book is all about. If you think suicide is the only way out, call someone—right now. I'm counting on you. *Don't give up.*

## YOU WERE COPING. . .

All these things and whatever others you may have done or felt are legitimate coping mechanisms. They are your survival skills. You do not need to feel guilty about them. Whatever you may have done to cope with the abuse does not make you responsible for the abuse.

You may be saying, "Yeah, well, you don't know all the things I did. So there's no way you can say I'm not responsible."

Wrong! Even without knowing what you did to survive—and that's what it was: surviving—I can say, along with hundreds of experts in the field of sexual abuse, you were not responsible for the abuse. You are a person of value and worth. You don't deserve to be punished, blamed, or hurt.

You deserve a life free of abuse. You also deserve all the future possibilities your life holds. So let's make way for your future by sorting through some of the issues you may be trying to deal with.

# 10

## Making Way for Your Future

*This has affected everything. I think about it every day of my life.*

YVONNE, SIXTEEN-YEAR-OLD ABUSED BY UNCLE

**S**EXUAL ABUSE OF ANY KIND can have a tremendous impact on the lives of its victims. It can act like a cancer that invades every aspect of your life, your thinking, your feeling and acting. The fallout from the abuse will not just go away, fade into the sunset, or stop when the abuse does. Incest and sexual abuse can be overwhelmingly destructive to a person's life.

The good news is that it doesn't have to be that way forever. You can do something to control how the abuse is going to affect your life. You can rebuild and heal. You can take control of your future.

Let's make way for your future by looking at some of the issues you may be dealing with. Keep in mind that this book can do only so much in helping you sort through these issues. Therapy (individual, group, whatever) is really the best place to deal with this stuff once and for all. But here are some important points to start with.

## FLASHBACKS

One day, you may be walking along and see someone who looks like the person who abused you. All of a sudden, you're shaking, you can't breathe, your heart is racing, and you feel like you're going to crack into a million pieces. Welcome to the world of flashbacks.

They can come without warning. They can be caused by anything.

When I see any kind of blue truck, I start walking fast.
NICKY, FIFTEEN-YEAR-OLD ABUSED BY MAINTENANCE MAN

When I smell coffee brewing or cigarettes, I expect my father to appear.
BRIANNA, FIFTEEN-YEAR-OLD ABUSED BY STEPFATHER

My boyfriend says, "Come here, I want to love on you." I had to tell him to stop. That's exactly what my father used to say. It makes my skin crawl.
MELINDA, FIFTEEN-YEAR-OLD ABUSED BY STEPFATHER

Flashbacks can be like a low-grade anxiety or they can transport you back to a specific incident of abuse. Suddenly, you can picture the type of clothing the abuser was wearing, the room where the abuse was happening, whether the window was open, and the color of the furniture in the room.

Other times, flashbacks are just an image of the abuser and an overwhelming sense of fear. Some victims see only the abuser surrounded by a black fog. Others don't have a visual flashback but rather a feeling flashback. They begin to tremble; they break out in a sweat and want to crawl behind furniture to hide.

Remembering how things tasted or smelled is not uncommon in a flashback. Remembering physical feelings can also happen—like how the rug felt against your back or the feel of the clothing you had on.

Flashbacks can be tremendously powerful and sometimes you must exert a huge amount of will to come back to the present. As weird as it seems, while the flashback is happening, you may still be quite capable of carrying on a conversation, driving a car, or listening to the radio. Other times, the entire present is forgotten and you are totally immersed in the past of the flashback. Flashbacks can be very frightening—not just the emotions you experience during them, but the fact that they can come over you so quickly and have such control over you.

There's really no way to avoid flashbacks. The best thing to do is to realize that what is happening is a flashback and that it will end. Try not to panic. Keep reminding yourself that this is a flashback, a memory, not the actual event of abuse; it can't hurt you. You've already lived through the worst: the abuse. You *can* live through the memory. Eventually, flashbacks subside and occur less frequently.

## A SENSE OF LOSS

As I have talked to survivors, both adult and teen, I have heard one common theme over and over: I've lost so much; I've been cheated. There's no question that sexual offenders are thieves. They rob us of so many things that we have a right to own.

In every step of the healing journey, you get to make a choice: fall into the pit of self-pity and stay there or spend a little time in the pit of self-pity and then *move on*. So let's look at what may have been lost in your life. It's okay to grieve for these things. It's okay to mourn the losses; but ultimately, we have to move on in order to survive.

### LOSS OF SELF-WORTH
One of the things I personally hate most about sexual abuse is the loss of self-worth—something that each of us has a right to own and that tells us, "I'm okay. I like myself."

When you are sexually abused you begin losing sight of your own goodness. Little by little, you begin to feel that you aren't important or valuable. You may have come to hate the way you look. Or you may have started hating your body, or the fact that you are a boy or a girl.

After a while, you may begin feeling like you're stupid, even though you get good grades in school. You may start believing that you're crazy or that everybody's life is much better than yours. You may even think that the world would be a better place without you. If that's what you're thinking, then read the words of encouragement on page 68 or the list of Blues Busters on page 66.

*Time's up!*

*WRONG! They get to decide for themselves.*

> **It's okay to feel grief, sadness, self-pity. These are all normal feelings. The trick is not to get caught in these feelings. At some point (and you get to decide when the time has come), moving on will be necessary to your healing.**

### We Need to Be Affirmed

Each of us has certain characteristics that make us unique. We may have great coordination, intelligence, a carefree attitude toward life, a stubborn will, artistic talent, whatever. Some things are just there when we're born. The job for parents is to take what they get in their child and make the most of it. It's not always an easy job, but it is the job that parents must do. A lot of parents fail.

If the people in your life are not helping you make the most of what you were born with, if they are not encouraging you and praising you, then it can be very difficult to grow up feeling good about yourself. If, in addition to that, someone is using you for his own sexual gratification, it can become almost impossible.

Put on top of all this the number you do on yourself, like "I'm responsible for what happened." "I should have stopped it." "I asked for this abuse." "I'm so stupid." "I'm a freak—this never happens to normal people."

And on and on. Then good-bye, self-esteem; adios, self-respect.

This is not the way it has to be. There are probably people in your life who *do* think well of you. Maybe it's a friend of the family; maybe it's a teacher or a family you babysit for. These are the people who are the "fair witnesses," as one therapist calls them—the people who see you as you really are and can give you a totally different message from the one the abuser has given you, or even messages that members of your family have given you. The fair witness can help you begin to look at yourself in a new light.

Instead of saying, "You must be blind" the next time someone compliments you on the way you look, why not just say, "Thanks." Instead of saying, "I can't do that" the next time you're faced with a challenge, why not say, "I can try." We're not talking major changes here, just little steps, one at a time.

### Rediscovering Your Value Is a Process

Finding your self-worth takes time. It's not like you can do five things in a certain order and you've got it. Getting in touch with your goodness and your importance is a major step in healing. Take it one day at a time.

Maybe you need to work on your body image to get over the idea that you are ugly or to stop hating your body. Try looking in the mirror each day and saying one nice thing about your face. Get a haircut or fix your hair in a new style. Look at one part of your body that you can look at comfortably and say, out loud, what's good about it (for example, "This is one great elbow").

Maybe you need to feel more in control of what you will and won't do in your everyday life. Try saying no to something you have a choice about and don't want to do (going to a movie when you really want to take a walk). See how easy it is? Okay, so it's not that easy. But the point is, it's one step at a time. One little thing after one little thing. Please understand these efforts are not going to give you back all of your self-esteem—it's a process, remember—but they are a step in the right direction. If you are in therapy (and I strongly urge you to get there), then your therapist or group can help you with other exercises in building your self-worth.

For more on self-esteem, you might want to read *Teen Esteem*, by Dr. Pat Palmer with Melissa Alberti Froehner (Impact Publishers, 1989).

The bottom line is this: you are a very valuable person. You have guts and courage and strength, perhaps more than most people. So focus on that. Stop believing what the offender or others in your life have said and start believing in the unique, wonderful, incredible person that you are.

## LOSS OF CONTROL

Children don't really have any way to control their lives. They are dependent on their parents and family members for their physical needs (food, clothing, shelter), their emotional needs (love, nurture, self-worth), their education, their ideas of the world, and so on. If a parent is doing a decent job of parenting, the child is slowly allowed to take over some control of his life, like picking out the clothes he wants to wear, which book to read at bedtime, what cereal to eat at breakfast.

Kids who are sexually abused don't feel they have control over anything. They are in a situation where they cannot say no and even if they do, it won't make any difference. These kids have to find other things over which they can have control. They may put their belongings in a certain order or have a special system for their clothes. They may have rituals like always brushing their teeth in a circular motion, or being sure to put the left shoe on before the right.

Other kids will gain control by acting out. By being a disturbance in school or getting in trouble with the law, some teens feel they are in control of their parents. Mom or Dad will have to leave work to come bail them out, or, at the very least, they will get Mom's and Dad's attention, even though it's negative.

Still other kids use food to try to regain control. These are the kids who are anorexic or bulimic. They either starve themselves using the mentality, "No one can tell me what to eat. I get to say how much food goes into this mouth," or they pig-out and then feel guilty and vomit it all back up. Eating disorders have very little to do with food and everything to do with power and control.

Needing to be in control is a common feeling for survivors of sexual abuse. Many feel a major need to be in control of everything and everyone. They feel threatened and afraid when they feel their control is slipping. Being in control can be a helpful way to cope with the abuse and can be an asset as an adult. Who knows? You could end up with tremendous organizational skills and run the country.

However, being the control tower does have a negative side. You can become rigid and always have to have things your way. You may not be able to admit when you are wrong. It can make you a lousy parent if you ever decide to have children. It can also make you a lousy friend if you have to always be in charge of where you go, what you do, and who you go with. Try to be aware of your need to be in control and keep it *under* control.

## LOSS OF TRUST

When that first episode of abuse occurred, you may have felt confused, maybe even terrified. You probably knew that something was wrong, something was not okay, but you didn't know what. It could be that the abuser told you that this was absolutely fine, but you couldn't tell anyone about it—that it was a little secret between the two of you. The abuser may have given you some good reasons for not telling. Or maybe nothing at all was ever said but the whole secretive nature of the interaction convinced you that things were not right. So there you are, feeling in your gut that something is wrong, but being told that everything is fine. Welcome to the Twilight Zone.

### Not Trusting Yourself

Because of years of being told "what you see happening is not really happening," you may feel that you can no longer trust yourself or your perceptions and assessments of people and situations. That's a very scary place to be. If you can't count on your internal radar, how can you possibly navigate through life? You can't. You end up bumping into things and having all kinds of wrecks along the way.

The message you've been given during the abuse is a powerful one: what is happening is okay, and if I can't convince you of that, then I will convince you not to talk about it.

You may have to overcome your feelings of being stupid for buying into that message. You may feel embarrassed that you weren't able to make the abuse stop. Hogwash! You do not need to feel bad about yourself because you believed someone you had a right to believe. You don't need to beat up on yourself because you trusted someone else's viewpoint more than your own. Remember, you were a child and kids are taught to listen to and respect adults and people who are bigger and more powerful.

What you *do* need to do is work on believing in yourself, your ideas, your awareness of situations, your feelings, your judgments. It's another process—not something that happens overnight, and maybe not something you can do alone. You may need the help of a therapist to restore the foundations of belief in yourself.

### Not Trusting Others

How do you trust anybody else if the people closest to you, the people who are responsible in some way for your well-being, education, daily bread, and shelter are the people who hurt you? The world goes on tilt when somebody close to you molests you. This planet becomes a very frightening place to be when you find out that an important person in your life is not trustworthy.

If you don't trust people right now, don't feel like a freak. Your reaction is pretty normal and appropriate. Trust is a very major issue for people who are sexually abused because sexual abuse is about breaking trust. Whoever abused you was most likely someone you trusted. If it was a person in your family, then you can probably relate to the trust issue very easily. What bigger break of trust can there be than for a family member to hurt another family member?

Learning how to trust again can take a long time—not because you're slow or because this is an insurmountable issue. Learning to trust takes time because you are learning to trust *human beings* and they can screw up very easily—and very frequently. When trust has been broken in such a major way as sexual abuse, you begin to want the people in your life never to make mistakes, never to lose their temper, always to think you are right, and to look a lot like Superman.

Sorry, but it's not going to happen. In the normal course of a day, people are going to let you down, break their word, hurt your feelings, and do all other kinds of things that don't encourage trust. The trick is learning how to trust people with all their faults and weaknesses. Be clear here: I am not talking about the abuser; trusting the abuser again is a different issue all together. I'm talking about your friends, adults in your life, teachers, all the people you come in contact with.

It's not easy and it does take time. But through good counseling and some trial and error, you will begin to find people who are truly trustworthy. Eventually you will give them the gift of your trust.

## LOSS OF BOUNDARIES

Another problem that kids who grow up in an abusive situation face is not knowing about boundaries. A boundary is an imaginary line that runs around you, your belongings, your feelings, and your actions. It lets people know they can go so far and no further. For example, if I stand too close to you while we're talking, I've stepped over a boundary. If I constantly come into your room and go through your stuff, I am invading your boundaries. If I interrupt you when you're talking or show no consideration for your feelings, I have crossed one of your boundaries. There are lots of little ways people can invade your boundaries and lots of big ways too, like sexually abusing you—the ultimate boundary invasion.

Unfortunately, boundaries are not something you're born knowing about. It's something you learn from the way other people deal with you. And if you're a victim of sexual abuse, you may not have a clue about how to respect boundaries— your own as well as those of others.

*A boundary says, "You can go this far and no farther."*

But more important, you may not have any idea how to *protect* your own boundaries; how to keep people from crossing over the line. You may not even know that you have a right to protect your boundaries, to hold up your hand and say, "You can go this far and no farther."

Do you have trouble saying no to people? Do you find that you do a lot of things you don't want to do simply because you didn't know how to say no or how to express your real desires? Do you put up with uncomfortable situations because you are afraid to speak up or worried you may hurt someone's feelings?

Well, believe it or not, you can say no to people, you can state what you want to do, even if it's different from what the group wants to do.

And you absolutely do not have to put up with being uncomfortable because someone is trespassing over your boundaries. Unfortunately, you may not know where your boundaries are or how to keep them in place. This may be another issue that needs some work in therapy.

## LOSS OF FAMILY

If the abuser was your father, then you may very well feel that you never had a "daddy." You may feel cheated and mourn the loss. If the nonabusing parent didn't believe you, you may feel doubly cheated out of parents. You now need to find a new way to relate to the abuser and the person who should have protected you.

Beyond losing the person who abused you, it's possible that you may lose other members of your family as well. If you've told about the abuse, your siblings or relatives may be taking sides. And they may not be taking your side! It may be a long time before you can all sit down for a holiday meal together. It may be never.

But part of healing is to sort out what you've lost in the way of parents or family and see if there is any way to rebuild some of those relationships in new and healthy ways. If you can, congratulations. If you can't, my sympathies. I know how hard it is to have to give up your family to save your own sanity.

## LOSS OF CHILDHOOD

> The thing I hate most about sexual abuse is having my childhood stolen. There are entire years that I don't remember. Fourth grade, for example is a total blank. I can't even recall who my teacher was. It's gone, vanished, vamoosed.
>
> LYNN, SEVENTEEN-YEAR-OLD ABUSED BY BIOLOGICAL FATHER

Like Lynn, you also may suffer from memory loss of pieces of your childhood. Or maybe you remember every horrid minute of your childhood—you can't remember a time when you weren't being abused. Or there may be good memories mixed in with the lousy ones.

Whatever the case, it can hurt to realize that you lost something that every child has a right to have—a safe childhood. And there's nothing you or anyone can do to change that.

## LOSS OF INNOCENCE

You also lose your innocence when you're sexually abused. I'm not talking about the kind you find in a courtroom—the opposite of guilty. I mean the innocence seen in children who believe the world is a good and safe place.

When you are a child, the world is no bigger than your house, your school, and your front yard. Your main interest is in playing with friends and going to school. The world is a good place—*if* you are a child who has never been sexually abused.

When an adult introduces the world of sex to a child through abuse, that child's world becomes polluted and innocence is gone. This doesn't mean that *you* are polluted; it means your *world* is.

Innocence is also about not knowing, not being exposed to things, not having toxic stuff dumped into your life. Like I said, somebody polluted your world and now you must find the ways to detoxify it.

It only takes thirty seconds to change a child's view of the world as a safe place, filled with people who will love and protect him. Once that happens, the world is never the same again. Danger can be seen around every corner, bad things can always be expected to happen, and happiness is for other people. It takes a lot of work to change that worldview.

## LOSS OF DREAMS

All of us have goals and hopes of what we will be someday, of the things we will accomplish, of the fame we may obtain. But when you have to spend so much time trying to avoid being abused and then coping with the healing, you start to think that the abuse and its consequences are the only things in your life. You may begin to resent the amount of time and money you are spending on healing. You may feel that opportunities and chances are passing you by because you have to spend so much energy on the abuse.

Healing and dealing with the abuse are the most important things you can do for yourself right now. It may be frustrating to put your dreams on hold for a bit, but it's *not* forever; it's just for now. Your dreams and goals will still be there. They may even be bigger and better than you ever imagined because you have learned that you have worth and value and can do anything you put your mind to.

*I know my dreams are in here somewhere...*

## FEELINGS

Do you feel? Do you know what feelings are? Do you know how to identify and then express your feelings? Do you know the difference between depression and sadness? Anger and guilt?

Don't be alarmed if you answered no to any or all of these questions. Feelings become a liability—they can seem dangerous—when you're being sexually abused. Shutting down your emotions may seem like the only way to survive. You may no longer cry or let others know when they've hurt you. The only thing you may know for sure is that your insides feel scrambled.

### FEELING NUMB

Feelings can hurt. They can also be controlled. And being able to control something in your life may be very important to you. For a lot of reasons, numbing out may be the only way you think you can survive.

The problem is that the more you turn off your feelings, the harder it can be to turn them back on. And there will be a day in your life when you are going to experience something that you want to feel, like falling in love, giving birth, loving a child. So don't kid yourself that life is fine lived as a nonfeeling zombie. Recognize that the feelings are going to have to be turned back on at some point. You may find that therapy is the best way to do this.

### FEELING "NUTS"

It is not unusual to have a lot of conflicting emotions going on. You can feel absolute rage at the abuser and still have feelings of love for him or her. You may be totally depressed and almost suicidal one hour and the next feel terrific. Having a roller coaster where your emotions used to be is all part and parcel of dealing with the abuse.

Don't let these conflicting feelings make you nuts. You're not crazy and you're not alone. Most of the feelings you have and the thoughts you think are similar to those of other people who have been sexually abused.

### FEELING GRIEF

Sometimes grief just hits you like a tidal wave. Out of nowhere it comes crashing down on you. You may spend a good portion of your days wanting to cry or simply feeling like a blanket of sadness is draped over you.

There's a lot to grieve. It's okay to cry about the abuse, to mourn the losses in your life, to be sad knowing that things are not the way you wanted them to be. Grief is a very normal response to what's happening.

Keep in mind that grieving, like healing, is done on your own timetable, in your own way. You may not be able to cry about any of this right now. You may need to stay totally dry-eyed and closed up. That's okay, too. Just don't be surprised if a year or two from now, you want to cry all the time. Grief will eventually come to you. Try to recognize it for what it is and allow it to happen.

Grief may not come to you until you feel safe in the world you have created for yourself, or until you have found a safe relationship with a therapist, or until you have done some healing. Remember, deal with it when *you* are ready. But be sure to deal with it.

## FEELING ON GUARD

When you learn that the world can be dangerous, you may develop a sixth-sense or a radar that helps you get through your day safely. (Therapists call this *hypervigilance*.) If you know where the abuser is at all times, what kind of mood he or she is in, and what events may occur to change that mood, then you can figure out a plan of action to keep yourself safe. Many people who are sexually abused talk about this "tuning in" to what's going on around them.

This awareness of everything and everyone can also follow you out into the world. You may instantly know when people are lying to you or not telling you the whole story. Or you may be super-aware of other people's pain and hurt. Or you may be very good at anticipating the needs and moods of other people.

One therapist I know calls it, "living in the subterranean levels of life." It's the ability and the necessity to see what's going on under the surface of everything so that you can be aware of danger and provide yourself with an escape route.

This method of coping can serve you well in later life. Some people feel they have psychic powers; others use their radar to their advantage in professions like counseling, detective work, journalism, medical fields, and human resources programs.

This ability can also drive you nuts. Being tuned into everyone and everything is exhausting. Additionally, if you have always "tuned in" to look for the negative in a situation, you may find that you see only negative things in people and events. This is a skill that you need to learn how to control, how to turn off and on.

## FEELING ANGER

> I remember one night when I sat out on the back steps crying and thinking it would be so easy to get a butcher knife and go upstairs and kill both of them . . . my mother and father . . . so easy.
>
> ROBERT, FOURTEEN-YEAR-OLD ABUSED BY BIOLOGICAL FATHER

Anger can be a very scary emotion, especially when it's directed at someone close to us. Most kids can't even begin to think about saying to the abuser:

*"I hate your guts."*

*"If I had a gun, I'd kill you."*

*"You are a slimeball, a worm, and I will never speak to you again."*

*"You are responsible for what happened, not me. And I hate the fact that you made me think it was my fault."*

*"Somebody ought to castrate you."*

*"I do not love you."*

If the abuser is a parent or a family member, it may be even harder to say these things. After all, you have to live with that person; you may depend on her for your food, clothing, and shelter. Additionally, you may simply not want to believe that someone in your family, someone who should love you and care about you did this to you. Most of us want to believe that our family members are decent people and have our best interests at heart. If you start thinking these horrible things about the abuser, then you won't be able to believe that anymore. Very scary stuff.

If the abuser was outside your family, it may be just as hard to scream these things at that person. You may be asking yourself if it's really possible that this fine upstanding person was wrong, or that you, a mere kid, could ever be right.

If you're religious, you may have been taught, "Honor thy father and thy mother." If you grew up in a household with a domineering father and he is the one who abused you, you were taught that what he says goes . . . and it did. If you're a girl, you may believe that you should be understanding and polite about this whole thing and let it go with a "that's okay." If you're a guy, you may believe that you can't get angry unless you can back up your anger with a display of force. But you're only fourteen and the abuser is double your size.

As you can see, there are a lot of different reasons you may have suppressed your anger and rage. It can be a lot easier, and not nearly so scary, just to be angry—angry

at yourself, your friends, your life. Angry at everybody except the abuser.

You may not even be aware that you are angry at the abuser. You may think that you have processed what happened and understand that the abuser has a sickness and needs help, not anger. But stop and give it a second thought. Think about all the things that you get angry about, the things that make you see red. Do you ever feel like you're overreacting to something? Like you're going around the bend over something minor?

I'm not talking about the abuse or being a victim. I'm talking about the little things in life: someone butting ahead of you in a line, losing your homework, not being picked for the school play, a friend who forgets to give you a call. These are not life-threatening issues, but your response may be one of absolute rage. And you may wonder why you get so angry over little things.

Chances are it's because of the rage you feel over what happened to you. This rage may have no place to go, no healthy way to be expressed. You may be afraid that your anger is so great it will be destructive and that if you let it out, no one will be able to survive it.

Well, the good news is this: it is entirely okay to feel angry about what happened to you—to feel rage at what has been done to you. But that anger and rage must be directed at the abuser in a nondestructive, nonviolent way.

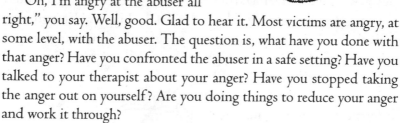

"Oh, I'm angry at the abuser all right," you say. Well, good. Glad to hear it. Most victims are angry, at some level, with the abuser. The question is, what have you done with that anger? Have you confronted the abuser in a safe setting? Have you talked to your therapist about your anger? Have you stopped taking the anger out on yourself? Are you doing things to reduce your anger and work it through?

There is a difference between identifying the anger and being able to do something about it. If you have not told, nor dealt with the abuse in a counseling setting, you may get stuck here. The only way to move on is to focus the anger in a healthy way on the abuser.

This may be a new concept for you, putting "healthy" and "anger" in the same sentence. Many people believe that anger is a very negative emotion or they are taught that they don't have the "right" to be angry about anything.

Not so. Anger can be a very healing emotion and a very necessary emotion to experience. Here are some healthy ways to handle your anger.

## Write It Down

Find a secure place for your writings and compose a letter to the abuser. Write a lot of letters. You don't have to mail them; just write down your thoughts and feelings.

Every time you feel the anger boiling up and you want to take it out on yourself, don't. Put it down on paper. If writing doesn't work for you, then put it on tape. Keep an anger tape going and voice all your rage. You never have to give it to the abuser or let anyone know that it exists; just write it or tape it. You will be surprised how much relief you can get from this.

## Role Playing

If you are in therapy (a very healthy place to be), then your therapist or group can help you get out your anger. You can role play, which means  you use an empty chair or your therapist as the abuser and then you *act out* all your anger at the abuser. You can scream, jump up and down, swear, whatever. The whole idea is to open the wound and let the anger out rather than holding it inside and allowing it to infect you.

### Exercise

Many kids (and adults, too) find it helpful to do some sort of exercise when the anger begins to bubble up. You can jog, walk, ride a bike, play a sport, punch a punching bag—whatever. Burn off the anger as well as some calories.

### Confrontation

If you're in therapy, you may get to a point where you and your therapist decide that confronting the abuser is in your best interest. This would be done in a therapy session with a trained therapist present to make sure everybody stays safe. *This is not something you should do on your own, especially if the abuser has been known to be violent.*

Right now, you may be saying, "Yeah, right. I'll just sit there and tell my mother, 'I hate you.' Then she'll start to cry and tell me I'm all she has, and then I'll get sucked right back in again."

Wrong! You don't have to get sucked back in again. Let your anger help you to avoid being a victim. Let it be a memory jogger so that when the abuser starts giving all kinds of excuses for why she abused you, you will remember that there is no excuse for sexually abusing a child. Whatever threats the abuser holds over your head, "I'll kill myself if you leave me;" "I won't be able to live if I don't have your love;" whatever her game is, you do not have to play. It won't be easy not to fall back into old habits or responses. But your therapist or group can help you with some responses and encourage you to remain strong.

You may be thinking, "You gotta be kidding me. If I vented all that anger, I'd end up killing her." Anger and violence are not the same thing. Read that again: *anger and violence are not the same thing.* You do not have to show anger in a physical way.

This may not be your experience in life: You may have seen anger expressed only through beating, punching, or throwing things. But you can be angry and not hit, slap, kick, or kill. Anger can be expressed forcefully and firmly without violence.

It is very important that you get in touch with your anger; otherwise you may start taking it out on other people—a younger sibling or relative, the kids you babysit, your friends, your boyfriend or girlfriend, or later in life on your husband or wife or your own children.

The other person who is in danger from your anger is you. You may be turning your anger on yourself in many ways and they all need to stop. You are not the one who caused this abuse. You are not the one who did wrong. You are not the one you should be angry at. (If you're hurting yourself, read about self-mutilation on page 140 and learn how to stop.)

## OTHER ISSUES

The issues we've discussed in this chapter are by no means the only ones you will ever have to deal with. As you go through your life, you'll find that new issues can crop up with each new life passage: graduating, choosing a career, getting married, having children, children going off to school, success or disappointment in your career, deciding what to do with your life once you retire. All these passages can bring up either new issues or pieces of old issues that have to be dealt with.

I've tried to touch the most common issues that kids have to deal with when they've been sexually abused. As you get older, you may find it helpful to read other books that will discuss issues that adult survivors have to face. A good one for adult women is *The Courage to Heal* by Ellen Bass and Laura Davis (HarperCollins, 1988). A good book for adult men is *Victims No Longer* by Mike Lew (HarperCollins, 1988).

On the other hand, if you have a major issue in your life right now that isn't listed in this book, don't freak. You are not abnormal or weird. I just simply haven't covered it in this book. Talk to your counselor, therapist, or group about it. They can help.

# 11

## Forgiving—Will You or Won't You?

*Have I forgiven the abuser? No way! Some things are simply unforgivable.*

ANNA, TWENTY-FIVE-YEAR-OLD ABUSED BY BIOLOGICAL FATHER

*I can't forgive him. Because then he'll think everything's okay, like it was no big deal.*

KATE, SEVENTEEN-YEAR-OLD ABUSED BY GRANDFATHER

*Oh, sure. I forgave my sister when she told me how sorry she was. It was obvious she felt really bad about what she had done.*

GEOFFREY, TWENTY-YEAR-OLD ABUSED BY OLDER SISTER

**I** **KNOW YOU MAY** have no interest in the topic of forgiveness. I know you may have been told you *have* to forgive or you won't be healed. Maybe, like Anna, you feel that "some things are unforgivable." But I want you to read this section as if you've never heard the word *forgiveness* before. We are not going to talk about "have to's" and "shoulds." We are going to talk about what forgiveness is and what it isn't as well as what it can do *for you.*

You probably never thought about forgiveness as being something you do for yourself. Most likely, you always thought it was something you *had* to do for the abuser. Well, keep reading. That's just the beginning of looking at forgiveness in a new way.

## WHAT FORGIVENESS IS NOT

There are many myths out there about forgiveness. Let's take a look at some of the things forgiveness is not.

### FORGIVENESS IS NOT THE FIRST THING YOU DO

You'll notice that this chapter on forgiveness is toward the end of the book. Forgiveness is not an issue that should be addressed in the early stages, or even the middle stages, of recovery and healing. Forgiveness is one of the very last issues that survivors look at. And that's the way it should be.

If someone is telling you that you have to forgive very soon after you've told about the abuse, find someone else to talk to. Forgiveness happens *after* identifying the hurt, *after* confronting the person who hurt you, *after* the anger about the hurt is let loose, and *after* the hurter acknowledges the wrong. Forgiveness is way down the road.

*Forgiveness*
*does not*
- *Happen first*
- *Happen easily*
- *Happen quickly*
- *Mean forgetting*
- *Mean excusing*
- *Mean trusting*
- *Make you weak*
- *Make you unsafe*
- *Have a timetable*

## FORGIVENESS IS NOT DONE ALL AT ONCE

Forgiveness doesn't happen in one sitting, one conversation, one responsibility session, one meeting with a therapist or minister or rabbi. Forgiveness takes time. It is a process with many steps. And when it occurs before its time, then it's "false forgiveness" or "cheap grace."

## FORGIVENESS IS NOT EASY

People often say, forgiveness is about will—if you *really* want to forgive you can. Not so. Forgiveness does not come naturally to us humans and it is probably one of the hardest things we can choose to do. It is much easier to wallow in self-pity, to feed our anger and rage, to plot ways to get even with the person who hurt us. Making the choice to let go of this stuff can be really tough. In making that choice, it may help to remember that it's hurting you more than anyone else.

## FORGIVENESS DOES NOT MEAN FORGETTING

This is probably the biggest myth out there about forgiveness. Many people think that if they forgive someone who wrongs them, they have to forget that a wrong ever occurred. This is not true. Forgetting, wiping the event from your memory, is impossible. It can't be done. No matter how much therapy you have, no matter how much time passes, there will always be a residue of memory of the abuse. The trick is to learn how to let go of the emotions surrounding the memory so that it no longer has the power to hurt you.

Sometimes it's not so much the fact of the abuse that eats us up, but rather the emotions surrounding the fact of the abuse: the rage, the fear, the intimidation, the betrayal, the loss. Letting go, not dwelling on, not obsessing about, not looking back, not getting hooked by all these emotions is the hard work of forgiveness.

## FORGIVENESS DOES NOT MEAN EXCUSING

Like Kate, who was afraid forgiving would send the wrong message to the abuser, you may worry that if you forgive the abuser he will figure that what happened was "no big deal," that it really wasn't so bad. But forgiving doesn't mean pretending the abuse didn't happen or that it didn't hurt or that the abuser doesn't have to own up to what he did.

Kids who want to see the abuser punished are often told they are being vindictive or unforgiving. The most intelligent comment I ever heard about this was from a fifteen-year-old who had been brutally attacked by an acquaintance. She forgave the attacker but felt very strongly that he should be imprisoned for his full sentence. When she was asked how she could forgive him and still want him to pay a price for attacking her, she gave this response: "Just because I forgave doesn't mean that I have excused. He has to pay his debt. If a four-year-old child plays with matches, you'll forgive the child because you know he has to learn. At the same time, you'll punish him by a smack on the behind or by sitting him in the corner because he needs to learn that it is wrong to play with matches. He [the attacker] has to learn too."

Pretty smart stuff, if you ask me. Wanting the abuser to pay the penalty, whether it be prison, mandatory counseling, or separation from the family, is not in and of itself wrong or a barrier to forgiveness. The abuser cannot learn anything if he is excused from paying the consequences of the abusive behavior. Very often, the most loving and compassionate thing that can be done for an abuser is to hold him accountable for the abuse.

## FORGIVENESS DOES NOT MEAN TRUSTING THE ABUSER AGAIN

Some folks think that if you forgive the abuser, you automatically trust the abuser again. Absolutely not. These are two very separate issues. Forgiveness is like the broom that sweeps the debris of the broken relationship aside and makes a space where a new relationship can form. That doesn't mean that the new relationship involves trust.

Trust may be a goal of the relationship but it's not a given. Trust is something people earn and the abuser will have to earn your trust—which may or may not be possible.

## FORGIVENESS DOES NOT MAKE YOU WEAK OR PUT YOU AT RISK

People sometimes believe that to forgive is to give someone else the upper hand or to let down your guard. Not so. To forgive empowers you, the person doing the forgiving. Make sure you read that correctly: *empowers you*. It does not give you power over someone else, but gives you power inside yourself.

Forgiving requires choice: choosing to let go, choosing to stop obsessing, choosing to move on. These can be tough choices to make. It follows that if you are making these tough choices, you must be pretty tough, pretty strong, pretty powerful.

And as far as being at risk after forgiving, well, forgiving doesn't mean you go brain-dead and stop using common sense. Remember, forgiving doesn't mean trusting. Therefore, you may forgive the abuser, but you may choose not to spend any time alone with the abuser or allow yourself to be put in situations where abuse could occur again. That's not being unforgiving, vindictive, or mean-spirited. That's being smart.

Now let's take a look at some things that forgiveness is.

## WHAT FORGIVENESS IS

Quite frankly, it's easier to identify what forgiveness isn't than what it is. I think that's because forgiveness can look like so many different things. However, let's give it a shot and try to paint a bit of a picture of what forgiveness looks like.

### FORGIVENESS IS AN ACTION

Forgiveness is more than a feeling. It is an act of creation. And you get to decide what it will look like. As Clarissa Estés writes in, *Women Who Run with the Wolves*, "You can forgive for now, forgive till then, forgive till the next time, forgive but give no more chances—it's a whole new game if there's another incident. You can

Forgiveness is
• An action
• A process
• Something you do for yourself and your own healing

give one more chance, give several more chances, give many chances, give chances only if."[1]

## FORGIVENESS IS A PROCESS

There are many steps in the act of forgiveness. Some people do all of them, some only a few of them; other people go over the same territory again and again. There is no time limit or schedule to forgiving. You set your own pace, deciding which steps you can omit, which you must do over. Understand that forgiving may be ongoing in your life; some forgiving may always be taking place.

The most necessary steps or building blocks for forgiveness are

- Acknowledging that you were a victim

- Acknowledging and processing your anger and rage

- Acknowledging your right to expect things will be different and that you will not be abused again

- Acknowledging your right to pursue justice

Without these steps, you can end up with false forgiveness or cheap grace, which does a disservice to you as well as the abuser.

Another piece of the forgiveness process is putting things into focus. Moving toward forgiveness is like taking off old glasses and putting on a new prescription. By doing this, you can see things more clearly. By looking through new glasses, you see the abuse for what it is—no excuses; you see the abuser for what he is—no excuses; and you begin to realize you cannot change these two things.

You will also, however, begin to see the things you *can* change: how much time you spend thinking about the abuse; whether your anger is helping you heal or beginning to consume you; whether you have become bitter and vindictive or are moving on from the hurt. The new glasses magnify the possibilities that exist in your life and diminish the destruction.

Hear me clearly, now. I'm not saying *minimize, negate, excuse, underestimate* the destruction (and hurt and pain). I'm saying *diminish, lessen, ease,*

1. Estés, *Women Who Run with the Wolves* (New York: Ballantine Books), 1992, p. 372.

*make more manageable.* When that happens, many of the stumbling blocks like consuming anger, resentment, bitterness, wanting to get even, will fall by the wayside and you can move on with forgiving.

## FORGIVENESS IS SOMETHING YOU DO FOR YOURSELF

It's important to realize that forgiving is not just something you do for the abuser; it's something you do for yourself as well. This is important to remember because sometimes abusers don't want to be forgiven. They can't even admit that they have done anything wrong, let alone believe they are in need of forgiveness. That doesn't have to stop you from forgiving the abuser, especially if you can look at forgiveness as a way of obtaining your own freedom from the past.

Forgiveness is an issue pretty far down the healing pathway. Forgiveness that happens too soon may be false forgiveness or "cheap grace." But there may come a time when, in order for you to move on in your healing, you will choose to forgive regardless of whether the abuser is around to accept it or not.

---

## RECONCILIATION

People often think that forgiveness and reconciliation mean the same thing, or that if you do one, you must do the other. Another myth. Forgiveness means to give up bitterness or the desire for revenge, to cease to feel resentment toward someone who has wronged you. Reconciliation, on the other hand, means to restore to harmony, communion, and unity; it can happen only *after* forgiveness occurs.

Quite frankly, reconciliation isn't always possible. It isn't always even the best choice because sometimes abusers can be very remorseful, without having a clue about repentance. And you have to have both for reconciliation to take place.

*Remorse* is what the abuser will often feel when finally confronted about the abuse. This feeling sorry for what he or she has done can be very cathartic, very cleansing for the abuser. But it doesn't necessarily mean that the abuser will change. *Repentance*, however, requires change. Repentance may sound like a really scary biblical word, but what it means (paraphrasing from the Merriam-Webster dictionary) is *to feel*

*contrite about what you did wrong as well as dedicating yourself to stopping the nega-*
*tive stuff and changing your behavior.*

My point, in a nutshell, is that remorse is a *feeling* and repentance is an *action*. Remorse *sounds* like, "Oh, I feel so badly about what I've done, so guilty for the hurt that I've caused." Repentance *looks* like someone making serious and major changes in his life so that he will never again hurt anyone the way he has in the past. I'm not saying that remorse is fake or not necessary. It's often the very first step an abuser takes toward becoming healthy. What I am saying is that remorse is only the *first* step. Repentance is the *many* steps in the hard work of reconciliation.

Additionally, repentance has to look like something the victim can see. An abuser may work very hard in counseling to change and that change may be evident in her marital relationship, her work relationship, and her social relationships. But if the change is not evident in her relationship with the victim, then reconciliation cannot take place.

Unfortunately, some abusers can never make changes that will be visible to the victim. Sometimes that's because the abuser can't get past the idea that the victim is allowed to have rights and expectations.

> My stepfather thinks he should be able to discipline me. I say no way. I mean he doesn't even live with us and he's not supposed to have contact with me. But he says he's still my father and I have to listen to him.
>
> MARISSA, FIFTEEN-YEAR-OLD ABUSED BY STEPFATHER

Sometimes it's because the victim will not allow himself or herself to see the changes the abuser is making.

> My mother keeps telling me her boyfriend has changed. And he has done all the stuff the social worker said he had to do. But I do not want to talk to him, be with him, see him, and definitely not live with him.
>
> STACEY, FIFTEEN-YEAR-OLD ABUSED BY MOTHER'S BOYFRIEND

Sometimes it's because not enough time has passed and more healing needs to occur.

My brother is like, "Okay, I abused you, but let's get on with our lives." Well, sorry; it just isn't that simple for me.

BRYAN, SIXTEEN-YEAR-OLD ABUSED BY OLDER BROTHER

## RECONCILIATION CAN LOOK DIFFERENT IN EACH RELATIONSHIP

Reconciliation can look like the abuser and the victim choosing to live together in the same house again, or it could look like an agreement not to have daily contact but to have occasional visits. Reconciliation can also look like an agreement that the abuser and the victim live separate lives with no contact. The key word here is *agree*. Both parties must be in agreement about what the reconciliation should look like. It may very well be that the victim is the one who decides what reconciliation will be and the abuser must honor that. Regardless of who draws the boundaries, there must be agreement.

Remember that there is no drawing etched in stone of what reconciliation looks like. Like forgiveness, reconciliation can be a "work in progress." It can look like one thing now and something totally different as you get older, as you heal, as the abuser has opportunities to earn your trust (or to rebreak the trust). You get to draw the outline of what forgiveness and reconciliation will look like in your life. Keep your eraser handy, though. That outline can change a lot.

Now let's talk about one other person who may need some forgiveness.

## FORGIVING YOURSELF

Wait a second. Don't freak. Yes, I know I've been saying over and over, "You are not responsible. You didn't do anything wrong." So it's reasonable for you to ask, "What in the world do you mean I have to forgive myself. I didn't do anything wrong, remember?"

Yes, I remember and you are 100 percent correct; you didn't do anything wrong. However, do *you* really believe that or are you still beating yourself up about different things?

Come on now, be honest. How are you feeling about the abuse? Ashamed? Responsible? Still thinking you should have stopped it?

Then please forgive yourself. Allow yourself to believe the fact that the abuse wasn't your fault and that it wasn't within your power to make the abuse stop.

How do you feel about the drugs or alcohol you used to numb your feelings? What about the promiscuity you displayed by sleeping around? Are you feeling stupid? Cheap? Then forgive yourself. Remind yourself (as often as necessary) that you were coping with something that no one should have to cope with.

Whatever the issues are that you're still hammering yourself with, stop. Forgive yourself. Acknowledge that you did things maybe you wish you hadn't. Make up your mind that you're going to find more positive ways to cope in the future. And move on.

Self-forgiveness is freedom. Freedom from the lies you've been told, freedom from the feelings of shame and responsibility, freedom from the mistakes you may have made.

As Clarissa Estés says, you are free to move on with your life. So far your life may not have been a *"happily every after,* but most certainly there is now a fresh *Once upon a time* waiting for you from this day forward."[2] So forgive yourself and get on with your life.

2. Estés, *Women Who Run with the Wolves* p. 373.

# 12

## Sex—What It Is, What It Isn't

*I want someone to care about me. But it always ends up being sexual. Can't you just love somebody without it being sex?*

GEORGIA, FOURTEEN-YEAR-OLD ABUSED BY OLDER BROTHER

**S**EX. ONE OF THE MOST misused, misunderstood, and misconstrued words in the English language. Little kids giggle about it on the playground; advertisers use it to sell their products; victims learn it's something that can hurt them or they have to use to get what they want.

Entire books have been written about sexual recovery from sexual abuse so I'm not going to be able to cover everything in one chapter. There may be things you want to know about body parts, menstruation, pregnancy, or the how-to's of sexual intercourse that I'm not going to cover here. However, I've made a list at the end of the chapter of some books you can read to get that kind of information.

Another area that I won't be able to address fully is all the negative sex messages you have received from the abuser. And I won't be able to undo the negative sex messages our society dishes out on a daily basis through movies, magazines, music, and television.

What I *am* going to do in this chapter is get you to start thinking about sex in a different way. And we're going to start with the word *sexuality*.

## DEFINING SEXUALITY

Understanding our sexuality is a first step in combating the effects the abuse has had on our sexual identity. As usual, none of this happens overnight, nor is it particularly easy. However, it is probably the best gift you can give yourself—not your boyfriend or girlfriend or future partners—yourself. Because you and your ideas of sex are all that matter here.

Let's start with what sexuality isn't. Sexuality has very little to do with sex. It's not sex appeal or how tight you wear your jeans or the way you wiggle your hips when you walk. Sexuality is not about your genitals and what you do or don't do with them. Sexuality is not an action.

Sexuality *is* a feeling. It is how you feel about yourself, the world, the opposite sex; it's how you respond to people and things around you. It is wrapped around every part of who you are, which means that it is a piece of your intellectual, physical, spiritual, and emotional self. It's part of the package when you're born. It's not something you can buy, learn, or borrow. You've already got it, but you may need help in learning how to own it and use it in positive ways.

There are four things I want you to learn about your sexuality in this chapter:

1. *The intellectual aspects:* your definition of sex may actually be a definition of *sexual abuse,* so we need to redefine sex.

2. *The physical aspects:* sexual desire and urges are totally normal and not something to be ashamed of. Becoming comfortable with your body's sexual responses is important to your physical sexuality.

3. *The spiritual aspects:* sex can be the most intimate and private thing two people do. It can be an opportunity for deep sharing and connectedness. This can only happen when both people consider sex something valuable. What value do you place on sex? What value do you place on yourself and your right to say no?

4. *The emotional aspects:* feeling good about your sexual identity is an important part of feeling good about your self-identity.

# INTELLECTUAL ASPECTS OF OUR SEXUALITY

How we view the opposite sex (whether they are safe or unsafe), what types of stereotypes we hold (girls are always victims and guys are always aggressors), our beliefs about sex (whether it is good or bad), and our attitude about sex as power or a way to manipulate others (sex is a weapon) are all controlled by the most forgotten sex organ: the brain. I bet you never thought of it like that, but the brain is a frequently overlooked and important piece of our sexuality.

> **The brain is a frequently overlooked piece of our sexuality.**

I'm not talking about the sexual fantasies it can create or the pornographic pictures it can remember. I'm talking about the brain's power to rethink, re-create, and rewrite our view of sex.

## SOME NEW WAYS OF DEFINING SEX

Dr. Kevin Leman has written several books on relationships, families, and raising kids. One of the catchiest titles he's used is *Sex Begins in the Kitchen*. This is a book for married couples, but the premise is that sex is a whole lot more than the act of sexual intercourse. Sex has to do with love and commitment and honor and kindness and courtesy and respect *and* it starts well before you get to the bedroom.

> **Sex is not the same thing as sexual abuse.**
>
> **Sex is more than sexual intercourse.**
>
> **Sex is not the whole relationship.**
>
> **Sex is a piece of the relationship.**

Dr. Leman believes that sex is built on things that are displayed in a caring relationship in countless ways every day. Without these components, sex becomes so much less than what it was meant to be.

I want you to take a minute and think about some of your definitions of sex, some of your ideas of what it is and what it isn't. I've made a list of some things sex was meant to be as well as a list of some of the things it wasn't meant to be. As you read it, see whether any of your definitions of sex are in the "Sex was not meant to be . . ." column.

| *Sex was meant to be* | *Sex was not meant to be* |
|---|---|
| good | bad |
| fun | dirty |
| joyous | shameful |
| pleasurable | hurtful |
| safe | dangerous |
| private and personal | secret or furtive |
| full of "stops" | out of control |
| a gift | a weapon |
| a mutual agreement | a reward or bribe |
| something you do *with* someone | something you do *to* someone |
| a *want* to | a *have* to |
| emotional and spiritual *and* physical | just physical |

Pretty interesting list, huh? Have you ever thought of sex as joyous? Fun? Mutual? What about the idea that sex is not a *have* to or even a *need* to. Sex is a *want* to. Something that two people do *together* after *both* have said yes.

It's quite possible that your experience of sex is as a weapon or currency in your life. Read the "Sex was meant to be . . ." list once again and try to imagine thinking about sex in these positive ways. Obviously, if you are still being abused, doing this is going to be pretty difficult. In fact, there is no way that sexual healing can happen while sexual abuse is occurring. So, reread the chapter on how to tell and get the abuse stopped so you can get on your way toward healing.

## SOME WAYS TO CHANGE YOUR OLD IDEAS
Unfortunately, just thinking or just reading are not going to bring about permanent changes in your attitudes and ideas of sex. Time,

practice, being intentional about stopping the old ideas in their tracks, and putting new ones in their place—all of these things will be necessary to bring about change. But they can be done and you're worth the time and work.

Here are some things that may help you get started.

1. Avoid music, books, movies, television shows, magazines, and people who reinforce the "sexual abuse" mind-set. Some of these are obvious: pornographic movies, books, magazines. Some are not so obvious. You may have to start consciously thinking about the television shows you watch, the movies you see, the books you read and ask, "What does this say about women? Does this treat all people with respect? Is the sexual interaction mutual or abusive? Is sex used as a weapon or a way of having power over someone?" If the answer is yes, then consider finding new kinds of entertainment.

And what about the music you listen to? Does it affirm women? Does it encourage males and females to interact in loving, courteous, respectful ways? No? Consider finding different music to listen to.

I know this may not be easy, especially if the majority of your friends enjoy this type of stuff. But there are other kinds of entertainment out there and not only will you be helping yourself, you'll also be helping others by not supporting the industry of "sex as a weapon."

2. Change your vocabulary. If you use words that put down body parts (words like prick, dick, boobs, tits, cunt, asshole) then make a conscious effort to stop. Use instead the biological names for them (penis, breasts, vagina, anus). It may seem like a small thing, but you'll be surprised how quickly you will become sensitized to the use of "sexual abuse" language.

3. Spend some time thinking about ways you once imagined sex could be, sex without abuse—if you immediately start imagining a scene in which one person has power over the other, then you can see that you have some work to do. Since sex is something that people do *together* not *to* each other, the scenario of sex as power or hurtful or shaming is obviously a sexual abuse mind-set. You've got a lot of negative images to overcome, so be patient with yourself if this doesn't come easily.

4. Talk about sex in healthy ways, in a healthy environment, with healthy people. If you're taking a health class or wellness class, you

may find this is a perfect place to practice talking about sex in healthy terms. If you're in group therapy, that may be another great opportunity to use your new vocabulary and work on re-creating new attitudes about sex.

5. And last, be intentional about getting information about healthy sex, sex as it was meant to be. In this day and age, not only is it politically incorrect to be ignorant of the facts of life, but it's simply not safe. Read books (there is a reading list at the end of this chapter), ask questions of knowledgeable people (your best friend may not know any more than you do), and then use that information to wipe out the old, negative stuff.[1]

1. Wendy Maltz, *The Sexual Healing Journey* (New York: Harper Perennial), 1991, pp. 104-107.

# PHYSICAL ASPECTS OF SEXUALITY

The physical part of our sexuality is not about the act of sexual intercourse. That's important, so make sure you got that. Rather, the physical side of our sexuality is about how we respond to touch, smell, taste, and our own sexual desires.

## WE ALL NEED TO BE TOUCHED

All of us have a biological *need* to have physical closeness and touching with other human beings. Yes, *need*. Research has proved that children who are not touched on a regular *loving* basis develop a syndrome known as "non-organic failure to thrive." This means that even though they are being fed, sheltered, and clothed, they are not thriving because they are deprived of loving, healthy touching. They can quite literally die from it. This is pretty powerful evidence that all of us have a built-in need to be touched in healthy ways. However, that doesn't mean the touching has to be sexual. It could be hugging, hand-holding, petting a dog or cat, cuddling a small child. All these acts will fulfill our need to have physical closeness; yet they aren't sexual in nature. So, hang on to the need for the contact but find new ways to meet it.

## SENSUALITY

Another piece of our physical sexuality is *sensuality*. This is our awareness of how things feel to our bodies. For example, silk feels very smooth and slippery, wool can feel rough, sweatsuits can feel soft, and elastic can pinch. A massage can relax our muscles and turn us into jelly. Having your back scratched gently can put you right to sleep.

Our sense of smell and taste are wrapped up in our physical sexuality too. Smell can be a very powerful trigger for either positive or negative feelings. For example, cookies baking can remind you of holidays, cut grass can remind you of weekends, and lily-of-the-valley can remind you of your grandmother. These could be either positive or negative reminders depending on what holidays were like in your house, what weekends meant, and whether you liked your grandmother. Taste can be a trigger in the same way: a positive experience or a negative experience.

## SEXUAL DESIRE

The other part of our physical sexuality is plain old *desire*, the urge to have sexual contact. There is absolutely nothing abnormal about having or not having these urges. Most people have sexual desires to some degree. It's what we do with these desires that separates people from animals, victims from abusers.

An important question for a sexual abuse victim to ask is, "Am I experiencing a sexual need that can only be met through sexual contact or am I experiencing another type of need that I've been *taught* can be met only through sexual contact?"

Too confusing? Okay, let me say it another way.

We've learned that all of us (including you) need to have healthy physical contact. The question is, when you get the urge to have sex, do you really want sex (sexual intercourse/contact) or are you looking for something else that you think you can get only through sex? There is a difference. Let's consider some of these other needs we confuse with the need for sex.

### I Need to Be Close to Someone

We all need to be close to someone. Remember, we can die without closeness. However, sexual contact is not the only way to be close to someone. Holding hands, being hugged, sitting close to another person, putting your arm around someone are all ways to get the healthy physical touch we need without dragging in sexual contact that we may not be ready for.

### I Need to Feel Special

Many times abusers manage to make their victims feel special and important in spite of the abuse. It can be very difficult to have that one "positive" taken away from your life; all of us like to feel special to someone.

You may be able to find other opportunities to feel special and valued. Your peer group may be a good place to start. You may find that you are special (in a healthy, nonabusive way) to a trustworthy adult in your school, or the parent of one of your friends. Just be sure to check it out. Don't set yourself up for more abuse or a breach of trust.

### I Need the Identity

For some kids, their whole identity is wrapped up in their ability to provide sexual pleasure. They may have been taught from a very early age how to satisfy the abuser and may have been praised and rewarded for "doing a good job." For these kids, part of their identity ends when the abuse ends unless they find other people to satisfy. They may become promiscuous and sleep around, or they may not know how to relate to people without being sexual.

Like everything else, overcoming this pattern is a question of educating and re-creating: educating yourself about what sex can be and re-creating your sexual identity to reflect your value and worth. Your group or individual therapy sessions are a good place to start with this.

### I Need the Physical Release

Kids who are sexually abused often feel that they are overly sexualized. They talk about how they "have to have sex" on a regular basis or they'll "go nuts." Well, you won't go nuts if you don't have sex and it's pretty normal to spend your teenage years thinking a lot about sex.

The best way to determine whether you are thinking about sex to an unhealthy degree is to ask yourself, "Is sex *all* I think about? Am I avoiding my friends so that I can be alone to think about sex? Am I allowing sex to overshadow my other activities?" If you answer yes, then chances are you are spending too much of your brain power on the issue of sex.

> *Change in our sexual attitudes, responses, and values comes through education and re-creation.*

As for the frequency of your sexual interactions, well, there's no tried and true number that's labeled "normal." Perhaps a better way to approach it is to ask yourself some questions: "Is sex the only relationship I have with this person? Am I using other people through sex? Am I using sex as a way to avoid other things?" If you answered yes to these questions, then you may want to consider cutting back on your sexual activity until you have had a chance to educate and re-create, until you've had a chance to learn how to be intentional about changing your thought patterns. In the meantime, you can use self-pleasuring (more on masturbation on page 195) as a way to reduce your sexual tension.

# SPIRITUAL ASPECTS OF OUR SEXUALITY

When people hear *spiritual* they often think *religion*. The spiritual part of your sexuality has nothing to do with religion. The word *spiritual* here has to do with your soul, your self, the deepest, most private part of who you are. It also has to do with the value you place on that most personal part of you as well as the value you place on sex and your right to say "no."

That's right; you get to put limits, create guidelines, take a stand, write your own ticket when it comes to sex. You get to decide what sex is going to mean in your life and what it's not. You get to say who you will share your sexuality with and under what circumstances. What a concept, huh?

## LEARNING TO BE INTIMATE

Many people think *sex* when they hear the word *intimacy*. But being intimate with someone doesn't necessarily mean being sexual with someone. In fact, it's a good idea to establish other kinds of intimacy *first* before you become sexually intimate. If sex is an opportunity for people to share from the very core of their being, then some trust and safety nets should be in place before that happens. Unfortunately, many folks jump right to physical intimacy and often end up getting hurt.

To avoid having your spiritual self hurt in a relationship, you might want to use the following checklist. It's kind of a progression of levels of intimacy that can occur in a healthy, committed relationship. It also can provide you with some guidelines on how to take care of you.

*Step 1. Intellectual Intimacy*—a sharing of your beliefs and value systems. When you and your date discuss the movie you just saw or an article you read in a magazine or the latest political scandal, you are being intellectually intimate. You are exchanging your ideas, philosophies, and values. This is often the first step in being intimate. It is also the step with the least amount of risk.

*Step 2. Creative Intimacy*—engaging in an activity that is difficult for you to do. Your girlfriend is a semi-pro tennis player, but you've never held a tennis racquet in your life. Allowing her to teach you to play tennis, or even just going to a tennis match and asking questions, is being creatively intimate. You're taking the risk of looking inept and ignorant, but because your girlfriend is important to you and because you know how much she likes tennis, you'll take the risk. This may or may not be a big risk for you. It depends on how well you handle looking like a jerk.

*Step 3. Psychological Intimacy*—getting past the superficial, the mask that we show to the rest of the world and sharing who we really are. This is risky stuff. When we share our emotions, feelings, fears, and worries, we make ourselves very vulnerable. We risk rejection. That's why this is the third step and not the first step. Building the foundation and trust for psychological intimacy takes time.

*Step 4. Physical Intimacy*—please note the number of this step. That's right—number 4. It's the last step in the intimacy ladder. Because physical intimacy is the opening of ourselves in the most personal way, it is the riskiest. Additionally, when physical intimacy (petting, necking, sexual intercourse) are introduced into the relationship, the relationship is changed and not always for the better. Therefore, you need to ask yourself, "Do I want this relationship to change? Am I ready to add physical intimacy to this relationship?" If the answer is no, then don't. Respect yourself and your needs enough to stand up for them. Don't compromise yourself; when you get right down to it, that's really all you have. So take good care of yourself.

You are in charge of your body, your sexuality, your emotions, your actions. This understanding can set you free from the knots in which sexual abuse may have tied you. It can give you the opportunity to set some standards, standards for you to live by and standards for you to expect from others. It also gives you the chance to decide whether you want to be sexually active. Not being sexually active *is* an option.

## YOU DO NOT HAVE TO BE SEXUALLY ACTIVE
You don't have to engage in sexual acts, sexual contact, sexual language, or sexual intercourse. You can take a complete and total vacation from any sexual interaction. Get a grip, now. I'm not talking for-

*BUZZ OFF!*

> **If you say "no" to physical intimacy, you may lose your partner, but you won't lose your self.**

ever. I'm talking *vacation*, a limited period of time, a chance to catch your breath, to figure out where you are with this whole sex business.

Refraining from having sex is called *abstinence* and it can be a very healthy decision to make. Abstinence is the only birth control method that is *guaranteed* to prevent unwanted pregnancy. It is the only *guaranteed* method of avoiding sexually transmitted diseases. And it is the only *guaranteed* means of avoiding damage to your sexual identity.

Don't think you can handle the pressure? Can't think of any snappy comebacks to say to people who try to tease you? Well, here is a list of things that other kids have found will pretty much put people in their place. That place, by the way, is outside your decision about having sex. Frankly, it's no one else's business but yours. However, for any ignoramus you may run into, here are some comebacks:

I make lifelong decisions with my head, not my hormones.

If you cared, you wouldn't dare.

Real men respect women.

I'm saving it for marriage.

I don't owe it to anybody.

It's a thrill that could kill.

I want you to love me, not my body.

Real men don't act like animals.

Any boy can, but a man can wait.

What am I missing out on? Pregnancy? Guilt? Hurt? Disease?

AIDS is forever.

If you really love me, you can accept "No."

I'm not ready for "Junior" yet.

It's just not worth it.[2]

## YOU GET TO SET UP SEXUAL BOUNDARIES

Now you've decided you are ready to move to physical intimacy, your partner is ready, and the relationship is ready. Then be smart and be clear about what that physical intimacy is going to look like.

Up to now, you may never have considered what you want or don't want from sex. You may believe that sex is something other people get to take from you. Not so. *You* get to decide what's best for you. You are allowed to put a value on yourself and your body and expect other people to respect that value.

Is your girlfriend or boyfriend doing something that causes you to have a flashback or to react negatively (maybe the way she kisses you or the cologne he's wearing)? Then speak up. Ask them to stop whatever it is. Feel free to explain why, or feel just as free not to. The point is, if the relationship is any good, your partner will respect your request. If your partner doesn't, I'd suggest you look for a new partner.

Don't like oral sex? Then you don't have to participate in oral sex. Forget that garbage that he won't like you anymore or won't go out with you anymore. Your boyfriend does not get to decide what aspects of sex you should or should not like. Only one person gets to decide that—you.

Is your girlfriend giving you mixed signals? She seems to be saying "come on" and then she gets uptight and says no. Talk to her about it. Certainly people have the right to say "no" at *any* point in a sexual interaction. (And I do mean at *any* point.) However, that could be really tough on you both physically and emotionally. So tell her. Come to some kind of agreement about giving clear signals. Set up some stopping places where you can check with each other about how each of you is doing.

The point is, physical intimacy is not just about a penis and a vagina. It is about two people with feelings and voices and brains who are

---

2. Reprinted by permission from Josh McDowell Ministries. Call 1-800-222-JOSH to find out how to order your own "I'm Not Doing It" T-shirt.

going to share in the most intimate way two people can share. And I'm not talking just sexual intercourse. Being physical with someone (hugging, kissing, necking) is all a part of sharing our innermost selves. Just make sure the person you're sharing that special piece of yourself with is going to give it the respect and care it deserves.

## THE EMOTIONAL ASPECTS OF SEXUALITY

The emotional part of our sexuality is the mirror we use to look at ourselves. It is how we view ourselves and what we believe about ourselves. Our sexual identity and our self-identity are so closely linked that one affects the other. Therefore, if our sexual identity is hurt, then all aspects of our self-identity will be affected.

> I felt so ashamed of what my coach did to me that I began to feel ashamed of myself, like I was shameful. I didn't want people to see beyond the front I put up every day of the "nice guy," the great student, good friend. If they saw behind that, they might see how disgusting I really was.
> HARRY, SIXTEEN-YEAR-OLD ABUSED BY COACH

Like Harry, you may feel that you are shameful and should hide behind a false front. In actuality, you may very well be a nice guy, a great student, and a good friend. But because you have been taught that you are sexually shamed, you may begin to see all aspects of yourself as shamed.

You may feel that you are worthless and deserve to be a victim, so you constantly allow yourself to be used. After years of abuse by her father, Meghan felt that way. She believed she was completely powerless and could never stand up for herself no matter what the issue—whether it was which movie to see, a disagreement with her older sister, or saying no to sex with her boyfriend.

It could be that you believe sex is dirty and bad and, therefore, you are dirty and bad. That's what Yvonne's uncle taught her. Every time he raped her, he would make a big show of washing himself afterward, because "she made him do this terrible stuff and he had to cleanse himself."

So take an eraser to the blackboard of your mind, erase the old information about who you are as a person—and specifically a sexual person—and start writing some new information.

## LEARNING TO LIKE YOUR BODY

Sexuality has its roots in our self-image, the way we feel about ourselves. How do *you* feel about yourself? Do you feel comfortable in your own body? Do you welcome your sexual urges and feelings? Do you like the way you look, walk, dress? Do you like yourself?

Liking yourself begins with liking your body and feeling comfortable in your own skin. We talked about this a little bit before, but I really want you to think about it. The abuse may have stolen any good feelings you had about your body. You are going to have to make a conscious choice to learn how to like your body again.

A good place to start is in front of a mirror—a full-length one if you have it. Now take a look at this amazing, unique person. Don't start with that "I'm a slug/unworthy/disgusting" business. I sincerely hope that if you've gotten this far in the book, you have begun to let go of that mentality a little bit.

Forget what the magazines and the movies tell you is beautiful. Instead take a look in the mirror and find what's beautiful in your reflection. I don't care if you have small breasts or a small penis or cellulite or tons of body hair or pimples on your back. There is still beauty looking back at you from that mirror. Find it.

Now I want you to start really looking at the different parts of your body. Look at your face. Lean into the mirror and take a good long look. Ignore the blemishes

Learning to like your body may take some time, but you can do it.

and take note of your eyes. Look at the color, the expression. Look at your smile. Ignore the braces. What happens to your eyes when you smile? Do they smile too? What happens to your face? Does it brighten? Do you look more relaxed?

Now look at your hands. Really look at them. What do they do well? Play a musical instrument? Draw? Comfort people? Build things? Create things? Write? Cook? Rub them together (put some lotion on if you want to). Feel the strength of those hands. Feel the warmth. Think about all the good things those hands have done and will do in the future.

Okay, now look at your arms. What have they done well? Are they good at giving hugs? Have they held babies or small children? Do they provide strength for people who aren't strong? Rub your hand down your arm and feel the muscles and tendons. Think about the good things your arms have done and will do in the future.

Are you getting the idea of this? You can focus on any body part you want to (yes, including your genitals—in fact use a hand mirror for a closer look). The point is to make friends with your body. I know that may sound weird, but up to now, you may have viewed your body as an enemy, as something weak and vulnerable. If your body responded to any sexual stimulation during the abuse, you may feel that it betrayed you when in reality it was just doing what it was designed to do: respond to sexual stimulation. So start wherever you feel most comfortable, but start learning to like your body again.

## LEARNING TO LIKE YOUR SEXUAL RESPONSES

The next step is to accept and welcome the sexual responses you have. Once you have made friends with your body, you can't keep your sexual desires and feelings as a separate reaction; you have to take ownership of them.

It may be that every time you had a sexual response to the abuse, your brain flashed a message: "This is my body's fault. It doesn't have anything to do with me." So you began to view your body as a traitor every time it responded to the sexual abuse. Now that you have made friends with your body, you need to accept your sexual feelings. They are totally normal, totally appropriate, totally okay.

Of course, my telling you this is not necessarily going to change your mind about it. So back to being intentional about relearning. When you have a sexual response, stop the negative thought in its tracks and replace it with a positive one. You may not be able to do anything more than say, "This is okay." No problem; it's a start.

Another way to become more comfortable with your body's sexual responses is to create them yourself. Yes, I'm talking about the "M" word.

## Masturbation

Talk about misunderstood words. Masturbation has gotten a really bad name. You may have heard a lot of wrong information about masturbation, like it will make you grow hair on your hand, your penis will fall off, you'll go blind, or you'll get pimples.

The truth is that masturbation is a totally normal thing for people to do. Masturbation is simply self-stimulation: this means that a guy strokes his penis or a girl strokes her clitoris for the purpose of sexual stimulation.

Masturbation can help you understand more about your sexuality and your body's response to sexual stimulation. By exploring your body in private and learning what feels comfortable and safe, you can help yourself deal with some of the negative sexual responses you may have been taught.

For example, if you tend to dissociate or have flashbacks during sexual contact, masturbation can help you learn to stay in the present during sexual stimulation. If you feel abused or that you don't have any control over your body's sexual response, you can stop self-pleasuring at any time to prove to yourself that you have control. Masturbation can also relax you and give you intense physical pleasure.

If you don't feel comfortable with masturbation or have religious beliefs against it, then don't do it. But keep in mind that many healthy, normal, sexually active people masturbate.

## THE BOTTOM LINE

In today's world, it seems you just can't escape sex. It's used to sell cars, clothes, fruit juice, and more. You can begin to get the idea that everybody's doing it and you're being left out in the cold.

Not necessarily.

People are beginning to wake up to the problems of premarital sex and the dangers of unprotected sex. Unwanted babies can happen and deadly diseases can happen. It's sort of like playing Russian Roulette: you never know when or what you're going to get.

People are also beginning to wake up to the understanding that by using sex any old way, we are diminishing its wonderfulness, joyousness, specialness. We are turning it into a commodity, a weapon, a payoff.

Sex was never meant to be like that. It was given to us as a gift; a gift that we can share with each other. It's not something we use to hurt each other or to gain power over each other.

Sex as it was meant to be includes things like love, commitment, sharing, trust, respect, honor, and courtesy. In this environment, sex is not a weapon or a "have to"; sex is a "want to" and is pleasurable for both people.

Sex as it was meant to be allows people to talk about what pleases them, what frightens them, what comforts them. Sex as it was meant to be is safe and based on trust and agreed to by both people.

If you're in a relationship (other than the abuse relationship) where your partner isn't interested in your sexual needs, where sex is hurtful, where you feel frightened or overpowered, then you might want to think about getting out of that relationship.

Remember, you don't need sex to survive and a little abstinence (no sex) could be really healthy for you. Healthy for your mind, your soul, and especially your body.

Girls, don't make the mistake of thinking that a guy will like you only if you put out. That is a victim's mentality, not the thoughts of a young woman who values herself and her body. No guy is worth your time if he's pressuring you to have sex.

And guys, you do not have to prove you're a man by going after anything with breasts. You too can say no to sex and wait until you have sorted through the abuse and started feeling like making love is what you *want* and not what you're *supposed* to do.

And for heaven's sake, if you've never had sex with somebody, you don't have to start now. There is no need to rush it. Your first time of sex as it was meant to be should happen in a safe environment with a loving partner. You deserve that.

## WORRIES ABOUT BEING GAY

Some kids have a lot of concerns about whether they're gay. Kids who are abused by someone of the same sex especially worry about this. As we've said already, our bodies are designed to respond to sexual stimulation—no matter the source. So if a kid has a sexual response to the abuse (like getting an erection or having pleasurable feelings) and the abuser is someone of the same sex, he may get very upset and start thinking he is a homosexual. Well, the news is: being abused by someone of the same sex does not mean you are homosexual and having a sexual response to the abuse does not mean you are homosexual.

At the same time, there are kids who *are* homosexual, have acknowledged it, and are learning to accept that part of themselves. Their worry may be that they were abused because they are gay. Not so! The abuse occurred because the abuser was out of control. It had nothing to do with who you are or how you act. Homosexuality is an issue separate and apart from the abuse.

Keep in mind that the teen years are full of worries and mixed-up feelings. Many kids who are not abused go through a phase of wondering about their sexual orientation. It's likely that your worries are totally in the normal range of teenage concerns. However, if you are concerned about these feelings and worries, please talk to someone—preferably someone like a therapist with expertise in the field of sexual abuse.

## YOU CAN HEAL YOUR SEXUAL SELF

Even though you may have had a horrifying introduction to sex, you don't have to continue to view sex as dirty, nasty, bad, hurtful, or any of the other negative ways you may see it. You can work out what's happened to you with a good therapist and go on to have healthy adult sexual relationships.

The key to doing that is to realize that you were a victim of someone else's warped desires and that you don't have to keep on being a victim. Any one who tries to bully, cajole, tease, or intimidate you into having sex with him or her is not worth your time. And if you are the one who is doing the bullying, cajoling, teasing, and intimidating, then you are allowing the abuse to control you. You have now become the abuser instead of the victim. If you are doing this, then get some help. You are simply keeping the cycle of abuse going and it needs to stop.

## MORE INFORMATION

If you have more questions about sex or just want more information, following are some good books for girls:

*Girls and Sex* by Wardell B. Pomeroy, Dell Publishing, 1981.

*Puberty: An Illustrated Manual for Parents and Daughters* by Angela Hynes, RGA Publishing Group, Inc., 1989.

*The What's Happening to My Body Book for Girls* by Lynda Madaras, Newmarket Press, 1988.

*You're In Charge: A Teenage Girl's Guide to Sex and Her Body* by Niels H. Lauersen and Eileen Stukane, Ballantine Books, 1993.

Guys can find more information in these books:

*Boys and Sex* by Wardell B. Pomeroy, Dell Publishing, 1981.

*The What's Happening to My Body Book for Boys* by Lynda Madaras, Newmarket Press, 1988

Both girls and boys can find information in the following:

*Sex Is Not a Four-Letter Word* by Jim Watkins, Tyndale House Publishers, 1991.

*Changing Bodies, Changing Lives* by Ruth Bell and others, Vintage Books, 1987.

*The New Teenage Body Book* by Kathy McCoy and Charles Wibbelsman, Putnam Publishing Group, 1992.

A word of caution about *Changing Bodies, Changing Lives* and any other book you read that includes information on sexual abuse and incest: depending on when the book was published the information may or may not be correct. For example *Changing Bodies, Changing Lives* says that sexual contact between siblings (brothers/sisters) is not necessarily harmful. We now know that *any* kind of sexual contact that *uses* one of the people involved is harmful. Just be careful about information you find in books that are not specifically written to discuss sexual abuse and incest; the information may not be current.

You may be able to find all these books at your local bookstore or library. If not, you can ask your bookstore to order one or more for you or you can ask the publishers if you can order the books directly from them.

THINGS TO KNOW

# 13

## What You Should Know About Offenders

I understand that it wasn't my fault. I understand that if it wasn't me, he would have hurt someone else. I understand that he's the one who made the choice to abuse. What I don't understand is why!

ROSS, FOURTEEN-YEAR-OLD ABUSED BY COACH

ONE OF THE BIGGEST questions kids have about the abuse is *why?* Why did the abuse happen and why did the abuser abuse me?

There is no easy answer. You can find lots of theories and reasons for why people sexually abuse kids—but these are only theories and reasons. They can help us to understand motivation and a little bit of the "Why?" question, but, they do not excuse the abuser from his or her actions and they do not take the responsibility for the abuse away from the abuser.

> **The abuser is always responsible for the abuse. Keep this in mind while you read this chapter.**

## FIXATED OFFENDERS AND REGRESSED OFFENDERS

Among all the ideas and theories about offenders, perhaps the most easily understood information was compiled by Nicholas Groth. He found that offenders can fall into two groupings: the *fixated* and the *regressed*.[1]

The *fixated* abuser is a person who has always had a "thing" about kids. From an early age in his or her own childhood, this kind of offender has had a sexual attraction toward children. He finds all kinds of ways to spend time alone with children so that he can be sexual with them. This person has difficulty making friends with people his own age and usually does not develop a strong love relationship and marry. He finds the company of kids more exciting than being with adults.

Sometimes, however, the fixated offender will marry a divorced person with children. It looks like the offender has established a normal, adult relationship when in fact, his purpose in marrying was to have easy access to children. This kind of offender requires specialized treatment to learn how to control his desire to have sexual contact with children.

The *regressed* offender usually abuses children who are within easy reach (like in the family) because of a sudden loss or change in her status. This kind of offender goes through the normal progression of being attracted to people her age, marrying, having children. However, when things change in her life, the regressed offender turns to a child in a misguided attempt to cope. Maybe the offender has been fired from a job; maybe she's getting a divorce; maybe a loved one has died; maybe she didn't get the promotion she was counting on.

This type of abuser is trying to deal with whatever pain, hurt, and anger the loss has created in his or her life. By reaching out to a child, the abuser can feel loved and special (children tend to give affection very freely, especially to people they know), feel powerful and capable (young children tend to idolize their parents), feel in control (children are taught they cannot say "no" and certainly not to a parent). By

1. Suzanne Sgroli, *Handbook of Clinical Intervention in Child Sexual Abuse* (Lexington: Lexington Books), 1982, p. 215.

using this weaker, more vulnerable individual, the abuser is building up her self-esteem and lessening her pain. In the meantime, the child is losing his self-esteem and entering a world filled with pain.

The regressed offender is a bit easier to treat than the fixated offender. There is a good chance that this type of offender will come to terms with his or her responsibility for the abuse and the devastation it has caused in a child's life.

## SO WHY DO ABUSERS ABUSE?

Many sexual offenders were abused themselves as children. Some were abused physically, some sexually; others were abused in all kinds of ways. Therapists who work with offenders often find that the abuser's childhood was less than wonderful. Therefore, as the offender grows up and becomes an adult, he or she is missing important pieces about how to relate to people, how to express love and affection, how to deal with anger and disappointment.

### SOME ABUSERS ARE TRYING TO FEEL IMPORTANT

Sometimes abusers feel so unlovable and unworthy that they will go to great extremes to feel better about themselves. Because children are so free with their love and adoration, the abuser turns to a child to feel special and important. Here's the story of a man who sexually abused his biological daughter:

> Phillip's childhood was hard. His mother got pregnant with him before she was married, a situation that was shameful for the whole family in those days. Phillip's mother and father were forced to get married. Because they were young and had very little money, they had to move in with Phillip's grandparents. Life was not easy.
>
> When Phillip was born, his grandparents and other relatives viewed him as a disgrace to the family. Obviously, it was not Phillip's fault that his parents had had sex before they were married and that he was born six months after the wedding instead of nine. But his family did not see it that way. Every time they looked at him, they saw living

proof that one of the family had brought shame and humiliation to the whole group.

When he was six years old, Phillip's father left. Not only was Phillip without any type of male role model but he also came to believe that he was the reason his father left. He figured his Dad was ashamed of him and couldn't stand to be around him.

He did well in school, became a pretty good athlete, and worked several jobs to help with the household expenses and to save for college. Never once did anyone say, "Thank you for helping out, Phillip," or "We're so proud of you." Never once did a member of his family come to a game to see him play. Never once did a male in his family take him under his wing and try to help him understand how to be a man. Phillip was always just "the kid," the person who was living proof of his mother's "mistake."

When his daughter was born, Phillip thought he had finally found someone who would love him just as he was and who would think he was wonderful no matter what. In a way, he was right. Daughters do tend to think their fathers are terrific and love them without reservation. However, Phillip crossed the line in his efforts to gain self-esteem. Instead of returning her love in a healthy way, he sexualized his relationship with her. He would fondle her when he tucked her in at night. He bathed her until she was ten years old, insisting that it was part of his job as a father. He would take her into his bed whenever his wife was out for the evening. As she grew older and developed, Phillip would constantly make sexual comments about her body.

Phillip was taking care of his own need to feel important, loved, and special without any regard for his daughter's needs or rights.

Phillip has been in counseling off and on for a number of years. He was never prosecuted and never mandated into a treatment program. The counseling he received is because he sought it out, which is to his credit. Phillip will be the first to tell you that what he did was wrong.

He fully admits his responsibility for the abuse. This is also to his credit.

However, Phillip still has a problem with boundaries, especially as they relate to his daughter, who is now a married woman with her own family. He has a difficult time respecting her wishes ("please stay out of my life"), her healing ("forgiving doesn't mean I have to have contact with you"), and her requests ("please don't talk about me to the rest of the family"). Phillip believes that his daughter is not making progress because she will not allow him to be a part of her life.

Most likely, Phillip and his daughter will never have a close relationship. But that may be what is best for her, and Phillip's task in life will be to accept that.

> *Some abusers are very insecure people. Being "intimate" with children makes them feel important. The love and affection children give freely to adults make this type of abuser feel special and loved.*

## SOME ABUSERS ARE LOOKING FOR POWER AND CONTROL

Steven is another type of offender. He abused three children: his ten-year-old daughter, his granddaughter, and a two-year-old girl that his wife babysat. He is now sixty years old. He is as thin as a rail with a face full of lines and wrinkles. His childhood was like this:

Steven's father left the family when Steven was very young. His mother had to work to make a living and there never seemed to be enough of anything to go around.

When Steven was six years old, he saw his mother having sex with his twelve-year-old cousin. He was frightened and confused. Then his mother began trying to engage Steven in sex. He found himself avoiding his mother at all costs.

When Steven was ten, his mother was remarried to a man who treated him like "an animal." After a particularly severe beating, Steven came very close to killing his step-father. He was twelve.

Steven grew up believing that the most important thing in life was power. If you had power, you could tell people what to do; other people couldn't beat you (like his stepfather did) or try to make you do something you didn't want to do (like his mother did). If you had power, then you were in control and could order other people around. If you had power, people would listen to you and jump when you said jump.

To Steven, power and control were everything. He was not interested in love or sex when he abused the three little girls—only power and control.

When a person grows up believing that the only way to get ahead in this life is to make people do what you want, he spends a lot of time looking for people to order around and have control over. A child is probably the easiest person in the world to dominate, order around, frighten into obeying.

An abuser who sexually abuses children because of a power need may become violent with kids, beating them into submission or threatening them with violence.

> *Some abusers abuse kids to feel powerful. This abuser is not looking for sexual pleasure but the satisfaction of being in control of another human being.*

## SOME ABUSERS THINK LOVE AND SEX ARE THE SAME THING

Sometimes abusers don't know that there is a difference between love and sex. They grow up without knowing that love can be expressed through kisses and hugs and little pats without having to be sexual.

They think that if someone is showing them *affection* ("love pats," hugging, kissing), that person wants to have sex with them. This perception makes it pretty tough for a child or anybody else to show this type of offender love because the child always runs the risk that the offender will become sexual with him or her.

> When Andre was five, his parents became unable to care for him. He was sent to a foster home. He never felt like he fit in and in a way, he didn't. He couldn't get along with his foster brother and sisters and constantly fought with his foster mother. Nobody ever gave him a hug or a good night kiss; they just weren't a touching kind of family.
>
> By the time Andre was fifteen, he had already been to prison once and was in and out of jail over the next ten years.
>
> "I never felt I had anyone. I never felt a part of a family," he says now. "Anger comes easy. Love is tougher."
>
> When Andre began dating and experimenting with sex, he believed that he had found love. He thought that he and his girlfriend were showing love and affection for each other when they had sex. He didn't know that they were simply having sex and that loving someone is a totally separate issue.
>
> He also never learned about the kind of love that a parent can have for a child, the kind of love that has nothing to do with sex but a whole lot to do with hugging and kissing and protecting and nurturing.
>
> So when Andre began sexually abusing his stepdaughter, he really thought he was showing love and affection. It took him a long time to understand that what he had done was rape and not love.

> **Some offenders think love equals sex. Therefore, when a child shows them love and affection, the offender thinks the child is asking for sexual contact.**

Human beings *learn* how to be affectionate, how to show love. Every person needs love; we can't survive without healthy touch and being shown affection. However, we need to be shown by example. If parents or other important people in a child's life take the time to hug him, to pat him on the back and say, "Good job," to tuck him into bed at night (without sexually abusing him), and to help him to feel the world is a safe place, that child will generally grow up knowing how to show love and affection. But if the exact opposite happens and that child is never *taught* to be loving, then he may not have any idea how to love other people.

### SOME ABUSERS ARE ACTING OUT THEIR RAGE

Then there are the kinds of offenders who are just out to hurt and frighten children. They take pleasure in seeing children scared and in pain. These offenders are violent, physically abusive, and very intimidating to a child.

Karen was a victim of sexual abuse at the hands of her brother, her uncle, and one of her cousins. Karen never told anyone about the abuse, and over the years, her anger and rage at what was happening to her built up. By the time she was eighteen, she was a volcano of fury ready to blow.

Unfortunately, a ten-year-old boy for whom she babysat became the target of her rage. She would take every opportunity to hurt him; she would pinch him, grab him around the neck, smack him, and twist his arm up behind his back. Eventually she began using sexual abuse as a punishment. Karen would put rubber bands around the boy's penis or threaten to shove things up his rectum if he did not obey her. Things finally came to a head when she twisted his arm once too often and broke it.

The doctor who examined the boy suspected that the broken arm was a result of abuse and not from "falling down the stairs," so he did a very complete exam. When he saw the condition of the boy's penis and rectum, the doctor knew that more than physical abuse was happening. He made a report and Karen was convicted of sexual abuse.

Because this was her first offense, Karen got probation with mandatory counseling. At her group therapy meetings, she is one female in a room of nineteen male offenders. However, that is the only thing that sets her apart. Like everyone else in the room, Karen was first a victim. But instead of becoming a survivor, she and the other offenders in her group became abusers.

Most offenders are nonviolent. However, it seems that more and more offenders are mixing violence with the sexual abuse. There is so much anger and such a sense of powerlessness in these offenders that they quite simply explode, doing serious damage along the way. Unfortunately many of these offenders were themselves victims. But instead of becoming survivors and learning to deal with the fact that they were abused, these victims are becoming offenders—and frequently violent offenders.

If you are even thinking about hurting a child, stop. Don't even bother finishing this chapter; turn right to Chapter Eight and how to find a therapist. Tell someone about your own abuse and make the choice to *move from victim to survivor, not victim to offender.*

More commonly, abusers who are acting out their rage by abusing kids don't seem angry. They act out their anger in nonviolent ways. Ed is a perfect example. He was never violent, never physically hurtful to his daughter, but he was working out his anger nevertheless.

For all of his life, Ed was put down. It became a family pastime. His father, mother, grandmother, and various cousins all found pleasure in cutting Ed down and telling him how stupid, incompetent, ugly, and hopeless he was.

When Ed married, he chose a woman who was unable to stand up for herself and he began to treat her the same way his family had treated him. He found fault with everything Nadine did— from cooking to cleaning to raising

their daughter. He would criti-
cize, belittle, humiliate, and con-
tradict Nadine at every turn,
often in front of their daughter.

In an attempt to avoid this
painful interaction, Nadine began
to spend more time away from
the house. This made Ed feel like
he was losing his power over her
and consequently made him even
angrier.

At this point, Ed began abusing his daughter, taking her into
his bed every time Nadine went
out for the evening. Ed's reason-
ing was, "I'll show her. I don't
need her. Let her go out with her
friends. I won't even miss her." He
believed he was "getting even"
with his wife when actually he
was expressing his anger and
rage at all the people and situations in his life that had hurt him.

> *Some abusers are
> taking out their
> anger and rage
> about their own
> abuse on a child.
> Sometimes these
> abusers are violent;
> sometimes they're
> not. Either way,
> children have no
> idea how to defend
> themselves and
> are perfect targets
> for this type of
> abuser. And the
> cycle just keeps
> going on and on.*

## SOME ABUSERS ARE INVOLVED WITH CULTS

And finally, there is the abuser from hell—the cult abuser. This type
of abuser may torture a child or torture other living things in front of
the child in order to scare the child into submission and silence. He
may be involved in ritual types of abuse that include connections with
a cult, like devil worshippers.

The most important thing to understand about this type of abuser
is that he or she is extremely dangerous and not likely to change.
While dealing with cult abusers is still a fairly new specialty, there are
people out there who can help you get safe from a cult.

However, I'm not going to kid you; getting free from a cult is not
easy. Rescuing kids from a cult can be risky business and professionals
in this area take a lot of precautions.

There are some commonsense things you can do for yourself in reporting cult abuse.

1. Don't broadcast your intentions about revealing the abuse. Take *one* or *two trustworthy* people into your confidence.

2. Tell a trusted adult about the abuse and ask him or her to make the report. Also, ask the adult to stay with you during the interviews with the police and child protective services.

3. After you have reported the abuse, take care of your safety. Don't go places alone; always travel with friends. Don't get to the bus stop first; make sure there are other people around. Don't get out of your car if someone suspicious is nearby. Don't ignore your gut instincts; if your body says run, then run. This is basic safety stuff which could be really important to your well-being. So use your head and take care of yourself.

Some abusers are simply unable to change. As I've mentioned, cult and satanic abusers are very difficult to change. A truly fixated offender can also be unable to change.

Many times, however, the abuser *can* change with the right incentives, treatment, and support.

Im outta here !

The cult abuser is probably the most dangerous type of abuser. His or her motivation can be a combination of the desire to have power, to hurt, to act out anger and rage, and to control through fear. The good news is that most abusers do not fall into this category.

## TREATMENT FOR OFFENDERS

The first thing to remember when talking about treating offenders is that not all offenders are alike. As we've already discussed, there are at least two different kinds of offenders and treatment is very different for each type. The possibilities for success in treatment can also be very different.

### FIXATED OFFENDERS

Fixated offenders can be very difficult to treat. Remember, this offender has had sexual urges for children for a very long time and these impulses and behaviors will be very difficult for the offender to change.

Treatment for fixated offenders focuses on teaching them how to manage their impulses and how to control their thoughts and actions. This is accomplished by rewarding positive behavior and punishing negative behavior. If the offender is able to divert or turn off the inappropriate impulses or thoughts, he is rewarded. If he does not turn them off and/or acts on them, he is "punished." It is similar to what a lot of us went through with potty-training: you "go" in the toilet and you get an M&M, you go in your pants and you have to wear the dreaded diaper. Okay, so it's not exactly like that, but you get the idea.

Another form of treatment that is having some success with fixated offenders is combining traditional group, individual, or family therapy with a drug called DepoProvera.

Curbing people's sexual desire through medication has been around since the 1960s, but only within the last ten years or so have concentrated studies been made with fixated sexual offenders. Not every state has this form of treatment available. Not every doctor or therapist is aware of it. Not every offender can benefit from drug treatment. But the initial results are very promising for some offenders to be treated with a mixture of medication and therapy.

### REGRESSED OFFENDERS

Regressed offenders have a better chance of recovery than do fixated offenders, especially if they are involved in a treatment plan that includes a number of different types of therapies.

Professionals working with offenders have found that a treatment program dealing with all the important relationships in the offender's life is most effective. This type of treatment can help the offender learn how to act in healthy ways with not only the victim but also with the offender's spouse, nonabused children (if any), and other significant family members.

### Separation Is Often the First Step to Health

Many therapists believe that the offender needs to be removed from the home as quickly as possible. At the time of disclosure or arrest, the courts may be asked by the child protective service worker to order the abuser out of the house. Even though separation is often the best thing for a family, it can still be very hard:

1. Separation can cause people to ask a lot of questions: "Why isn't your Dad living with you anymore?"

2. Separation can cause financial worries. It's expensive to run two households, one for the abuser and one for the family.

3. Separation can make the nonabusing parent very sad. If your mom is the nonabusing parent, she may miss her husband (or boyfriend). It may be very hard for her to stay strong and maintain the separation.

4. Separation can cause the victim to feel like the "bad guy." Everyone may be pointing a finger and saying, "It's all your fault."

In spite of how hard separation can be, it's often the best thing. All the family members have a chance to catch their breath; the victim may feel safe for the first time in months or years, and the offender may be relieved that he won't have to fight his abusive urges.

A temporary separation may become more permanent once the case goes to trial. The court may decide that keeping the abuser separated from the family should be a part of his or her probation. If that's the case, the abuser will not be allowed to be back with the family until the court says so. The court will decide when the time is right based on the information it receives from the professionals who are working with the offender and the family.

### Working with Professionals Can Help

One of the most important things an offender can do is to get into therapy. This is also important for the family and the victim. In fact, it's not unusual for an offender and his family to be involved in many different kinds of therapies. The offender could be in one or more of these:

- *An offenders' group,* meeting on a once-a-week basis or even more often.

- *Individual therapy,* where the offender meets with a therapist to talk privately about his feelings and to learn why he does the things he does.

- *A couples' group,* meeting regularly with his spouse to develop healthier communication, to learn how to share and manage feelings, and to reestablish trust.

- *Family therapy,* usually the last stage of an offender's treatment. This is an opportunity for the entire family to discuss their feelings of hurt and anger as well as their hopes and goals.

Obviously, an offender who is involved with all these different therapies would be one who has admitted the abuse, has taken responsibility for it, and is committed to getting back with his family. An offender who can't even admit that he has abused a child has a very long way to go before he can benefit from working with the professionals in the field of sexual abuse treatment.

## HOW WILL THE OFFENDER'S TREATMENT AFFECT ME?

A very reasonable question for you to ask, especially if you read the list of therapies an offender might be involved in. Noticed that "family therapy," didn't you? Family means you, your mom and your dad, your sister and your brother. Yep, family therapy includes you.

Well, don't get worked up just yet. Family therapy is one of the *goals* for an offender and his family. It should not start right away. The offender has to come to grips with a number of things first, like

admitting his responsibility for the
abuse, taking a hard look at the devastation and destruction he has
caused in the lives of others, and
making a decision to heal and to deal
with his problem. Only then can the
step be made to getting together with
the family and beginning to work
things out.

## FAMILY THERAPY CAN HELP EVERYONE

Therapists who work with families
where incest or sexual abuse have occurred feel that getting the family
together not only helps the abuser but the individual members of the
family as well. It's a chance for all members to voice their feelings, their
worries, their anger. Very often the kids who have not been abused get
lost in the shuffle. They can feel left out in the crisis of disclosure and
the tumult immediately following. They may be traumatized by the
sudden departure of the offending parent and may have little or no
understanding of what happened.

By having family therapy, all the family members, especially the
nonabused children, get a chance to say how angry they are about the
changes that have happened in their lives. They may
also point their fingers at the victim as the source of
the problem, but with the therapist there, those
fingers will get pointed in the direction of the real
source of the problem. (100 points if you know who
that person is—answer at end of chapter.)

I know!

## THERAPY SESSIONS BETWEEN YOU AND THE ABUSER

As a part of family therapy, one recommendation may be for you and
the abuser to have a few sessions together with a therapist. This is
often referred to as a "responsibility session." If this is more than you
can deal with, say so. But before you decide you can't handle it, let's
look at some benefits you might get.

### Hearing the Abuser Take Responsibility for the Abuse

One of the most important goals for an abuser is to understand that he or she was responsible for the abuse. The victim was just that: a victim who was in no way responsible for what happened.

Such a session won't occur right away or even in the first few months of treatment. It is something that the offender works toward, part of his or her process of healing.

Eventually, the offender and his therapist may feel that it would be good for the offender to tell you that he fully understands that the abuse was his fault, that you were not responsible, did not "ask for it" or "lead him on," and that he is sorry for what he has done.

Before you agree to meet with the offender, there are some questions you and your therapist need to talk about: are you ready to be in the same room with the offender? Are you ready to hear this from the offender? Will it help you? Will it hurt you?

> **Meeting with the abuser is a good idea only if it is going to benefit you.**

Maybe you simply aren't ready. That's okay. Even though we're talking about treatment for the offender, your needs and benefits have to be considered too. In fact, I'm going to go so far as to say that your needs are more important in the equation than the offender's. Think about it. What sense does it make for the abuser to heal at your expense? That's been the old pattern—the abuser gains because you lose. Let's avoid that and be sure that any decisions made about meeting with the abuser are going to be beneficial to you.

A responsibility session should also give you (the victim) an opportunity to say how angry you are about what happened, how mad you are at the abuser, how bad this whole thing has made you feel, or whatever else you need to say. If you're reluctant to have a responsibility session, think of it in terms of an opportunity to get a lot of stuff off your chest and a chance to vent some of the anger that's been building up.

You may say, "Huh-uh, no way."

No problem. It may not be the right time for you and that's okay. Maybe a responsibility session will never be right for you. Just give it some thought and understand that it may be an important step in your own healing.

*I don't think I'm ready for this.*

IMPORTANT: A responsibility session should only take place if

• A trained therapist is present

• The offender has been in counseling for a period of time

• The victim feels that it would be beneficial

### Hearing the Abuser Say "I'm Sorry"

One of the things that may come out of a responsibility session is the abuser's saying how sorry he or she is for what happened. That may be something you really want to hear, or it may be something that makes you really angry and say, "Sure, words are easy. But they don't undo what's been done."

Maybe you *never* want the abuser to say "I'm sorry" because you think that you will *have* to forgive the abuser because he's apologizing. Not so. Apologies do not automatically draw out forgiveness. That is a process, too. Forgiveness does not happen just because an apology is made. (More about forgiveness in Chapter Eleven.)

## YOU CAN CHOOSE HEALING EVEN IF THE OFFENDER DOESN'T

Some abusers will never heal. Maybe they are so entrenched in their negative behavior that no amount of therapy will cure them. Maybe they won't admit they are abusers or are unwilling to take responsibility for what happened. Maybe they simply don't want to change.

Whatever the abuser decides about his or her healing does not have to affect the choice *you* make about healing. If the abuser chooses not to heal, that choice begins and ends with her. You can still choose to become a survivor, with all that surviving can mean to your life.

If the abuser does not choose healing, it can make your journey tougher, but you've been through tough times before. You've been abused, remember? You can make it through healing.

Answer to question on page 217:
The abuser is always responsible for the abuse.

# 14

# What Friends of Victims Should Know

I didn't know what to do when she told me. I sort of stuttered that everything would be okay. Now I know how stupid that was to say. I went looking for books to read. You had to have a Ph.D. to understand the books out there. I just didn't know what to do.

ALLISON, FOURTEEN-YEAR-OLD FRIEND OF A SEXUAL ABUSE VICTIM

**I**F YOU ARE THE FRIEND of someone who has been sexually abused, then buckle your seatbelt, you're in for a bumpy ride. I don't say that to scare you but to let you know that hanging in there with your friend will not be easy.

You may realize that already. You may be having difficulty believing that the person your friend has identified as the abuser really did it. You may be saying to yourself, "Impossible. I know Mr. So and So. He would never do that."

You may be having difficulty with the reality of sexual abuse. It's one thing to hear about it on *Oprah* or to read about it in *People* magazine, and another thing to discover it in your friend's life.

Nevertheless, you will have to put aside your doubts and recognize that what your friend is telling you is most likely true and that sexual abuse *does* happen in real life. Do your friend a favor and believe him. It's the greatest gift you can give right now.

## THREE THINGS TO SAY TO A FRIEND WHO HAS BEEN SEXUALLY ABUSED

First, "I believe you" is the most important and best thing to say to a friend who has just told you she's been sexually abused. It takes a lot of courage for someone to reveal abuse. Obviously, your friend is putting her trust in you and your friendship. Be careful that the surprise of the revelation doesn't cause you to blurt out, "I don't believe it." Your friend may only hear, "I don't believe *you*."

The second most important thing you can say is, "It wasn't your fault." Believe it or not, many kids who are sexually abused think that they are responsible for their abuse. They think that they somehow caused it to happen. They take all the blame and figure they deserved to be abused.

All of this is garbage. The victim is *never* responsible for the abuse. The victim is just that, a victim: the person who was done to; the person who was used; the person who got robbed of some basic rights, like privacy and the right to say "no" and to have people pay attention. Your friend didn't ask to be sexually abused and she didn't "want" the abuse. What happened happened because the abuser was unable to control his feelings and actions. The abuse happened because the abuser decided that his needs were more important than your friend's needs. And that stinks!

> **Three things to say to a friend who has just told you he or she has been sexually abused:**
>
> 1. **I believe you**
>
> 2. **It wasn't your fault**
>
> 3. **You're not alone**

So tell your friend, "You realize this was not your fault, right?" It may be the first time anyone has ever said that to your friend and she may argue with you, may try to convince you that it was her fault, may tell you you don't know anything about it. Hang tough. The victim is never responsible for the abuse. The abuser is always responsible for the abuse. That's a fact.

The third thing you can safely say to a friend is, "You're not alone. This happens a lot. You're not a freak." This may be really important for your friend to hear. Say the statistics to him: one out of three women are sexually abused by someone outside their family; one out of four women are sexually abused by someone in their family; and one out of seven, maybe as many as one out of five men are sexually abused by somebody—all of this by the time the kid reaches the age of eighteen. This translates into a lot of girls and guys out there who have been sexually abused. And they weren't responsible for their abuse, either!

Your friend may think you're trying to say, "This is no big deal" when you state those statistics. Make sure you get your point across correctly. You're trying to let your friend know that he is not some kind of mutant. He is totally normal. What *happened* to him is the thing that is abnormal. The fact that it happens to a lot of kids will not take away the pain, the trauma, the horror. All of those things are very real for your friend. You just want him to know that there are lots of kids out there who have to deal with this garbage. Your friend is not alone.

Now that you know three things you can safely say to someone who is telling you she's been sexually abused, let me give you a list of things *not* to say.

## SOME THINGS NOT TO SAY

1. "I don't believe it." Basically, you're telling your friend that she's a liar, that her claim is so off the wall there's no way you or anyone else could believe it. *This is absolutely the worst thing you can possibly say.*
2. "Why did he do that to you? You must have led him on." What you're saying is that your friend was responsible for his own abuse. Wrong! Remember, the only person responsible for the abuse is the abuser. It doesn't matter how good-looking your friend is or how big a flirt he is; that has nothing to do with *abuse*. Always remember this is sexual *abuse*—not fun, not games, not something both people agree on. This is *abuse* and the person who was supposed to make sure it didn't happen was the abuser.
3. "Just don't think about it. I mean, there's really nothing you can do. What happened, happened. It's over now. Just move on." Unfortunately, a person doesn't just move on from sexual abuse. A person has

Some things not to say to a friend who has just told you he's been sexually abused:

1. I don't believe you.

2. Why did he do that? Why didn't you just say no? Why didn't you stop it? Why did you let him?

3. Just forget it and move on.

4. I know how you feel.

5. I feel sorry for you.

6. He is really scum for doing that to you.

7. Maybe you misunderstood what happened.

to sort through it, deal with the conflicting emotions—the rage, the grief, the fear. A person who has been sexually abused can never just close the door on it and figure it will go away. A lot of time and energy needs to be spent on healing from the damage that someone else inflicted on her life.

Your friend may even be saying this herself, "It was no big deal. I'm fine." This is not unusual. She may not be ready to confront the effects sexual abuse has had on her and may very well act as though she's simply going to get on with her life. At some point, though, she will have to face up to the stuff churning around inside. The trick is to allow your friend to do that in her own time.

4. "I know just how you feel." Trust me on this: unless you have been sexually abused, you haven't a clue about how your friend feels. You may think that you're showing empathy and being helpful, but you're not. So don't say this either.

5. "I feel so sorry for you." Ugh. The last thing your friend needs right now is your pity. You may not mean it that way, but it will sound like you are offering some sort of charity, or worse, patronizing him.

You can try to say something like, "I am so sorry this happened to you" which sounds a little different from "I'm sorry *for* you." But don't be surprised if your friend gets upset. Best to just stay away from the word *sorry*.

6. "I am so angry at him for doing this to you." "I hate her for doing this to you." These statements aren't a very good idea, either. You see, no matter how bad things were for the victim, many kids will come to the defense of the abuser if someone else starts saying mean things about him or her. It's difficult to understand how kids could feel any kind of loyalty to someone who hurt them so much, but it happens. If you start bad mouthing the abuser, you may find your friend arguing right back at you: "She's really not so bad. She didn't mean to hurt me," or "He's still my father and you can't say those kinds of things about him."

Don't bad mouth the abuser. Your friend may feel you are attacking her as well as the abuser, especially if the abuser was someone in her family.

7. "Are you sure you didn't just misunderstand?" This is often one of the first questions people ask a victim, so don't feel stupid if it's on the tip of your tongue to ask—just don't ask it. This question may hook into your friend's own doubts about his perceptions of what happened. For years now, your friend may have been trying to tell himself that he just misunderstood or misinterpreted what was going on. Finally, he has found the courage to tell, to say something about it; but your question can put him back to questioning himself all over again.

There are lots of other things you probably shouldn't say or do, but this list covers the biggies. Now let's talk about you and how you're feeling with all of this.

## DEALING WITH YOUR FRIEND'S REVELATION

The news that your friend has been or is being sexually abused may have put you into a tailspin. You may be tied up in knots with a lot of emotions or you may be trying to blow it off by shutting down all your feelings.

There are some right and wrong ways to *deal* with your friend's revelation. But there is no right or wrong way to *feel* about it. Put aside any "shoulds," "have tos," and "ought tos" and let's talk about what may be going on with you.

### I CAN'T BELIEVE IT

Many teens who have just heard that a friend of theirs was or is being sexually abused are dumbfounded. They have serious difficulty believing what they are hearing. (Of course, now that you have read the previous pages, you know that you should never say, "I don't believe you," even though you may be thinking it.)

Maybe you know the person who your friend says abused him. Maybe you really like that person. Maybe you're looking at your friend and thinking, "This doesn't happen in our neighborhood. You only read about this stuff in supermarket rags."

> *It's okay if you're having a hard time believing what your friend has told you. That's pretty normal.*
> *It's not okay to tell your friend you don't believe her. Do your best to listen to her with an open mind and to be supportive.*

It's totally normal for you to have difficulty believing what your friend is telling you. *Just don't say it.* Give yourself some time to adjust to this news. Listen to whatever your friend is willing to tell you about the abuse; don't pry. Try to see the situation from your friend's point of view and do your best to believe what she's saying.

A lot of people these days are saying that kids are starting to lie about being sexually abused. While I know that there *are* a very few kids who do lie about sexual abuse, the *majority* do not. When you think about the upheaval and misery that revelations about sexual abuse cause to the victim and the family, you have to figure that not many kids are going to lie about it and get themselves *into* trouble. Kids will lie to get *out* of trouble, but not to get *in* trouble. So do your best to believe your friend. Eventually your shock and disbelief will go away.

## I'M SO ANGRY

> "I was really angry at her brother. . . . I was so mad at him for violating [her]. There was nothing she had done. And like, she remembers them laughing at her . . . that really stuck in my mind because I know that really hurt her. . . . I'd like to kill him.
> ALEX, SIXTEEN-YEAR-OLD BOYFRIEND OF SEXUAL ABUSE VICTIM

It's pretty common for people to be angry about sexual abuse. So, if you're feeling angry about what happened to your friend, you're normal.

I have enough troubles without worrying about you!

Be sure to keep your anger under control. You won't be any help to your friend if you're in jail because you did something violent. You also won't be any help to your friend if she thinks she has to protect you from your emotions.

If, like Alex, you are dating or are romantically involved with someone who tells you she's been sexually abused, you may have more than the average amount of anger. Because you have loving feelings toward the victim, you may feel that it is your job to avenge her honor. Like Alex, you may even feel some violent desires and fantasize about doing bodily harm to the abuser.

Get a grip. Your anger needs to be kept on a tight leash. I'm not telling you to ignore it or try to stuff it down. What I am saying is you need to deal with it in a responsible way. Telling the victim all about your anger is not going to help her. In fact, it may even cause her more distress than she's already feeling.

Be assured that any act of violence can easily push her over the edge; so keep your anger to yourself or find someone else to talk to about it. This brings us to the next item for consideration.

### I NEED TO TALK IT OVER

You may feel that all of this is too much to handle. You may feel a real need to talk to somebody about what your buddy has told you. You may still be in a state of shock and need to share this information just to process it and absorb it. You may need to have someone listen to how angry you are that this happened to your friend. You may be overwhelmed with the idea that you have to do something with the information you have about the abuse. Don't let all this get you down. If you need to, talk to someone else about the fact that your friend is being abused.

However, don't talk to just anybody about it. Be selective in the person you find to help you. This should be someone who is mature and trustworthy and *not* the kind to gossip. The people at the party you're going to this weekend are not a good choice. Neither is the group you hang out with after school.

> *Use good sense and good judgment when you're looking for someone to talk to. Be sure you pick someone who is trustworthy and discreet.*

One of your parents might be a good choice. You could also consider talking to a teacher, a guidance counselor, a religious leader, or an adult in your life whom you trust and respect. Please pick carefully. Your friend deserves it.

This person can be helpful to you in sorting out your own feelings about the fact your friend was abused. He or she can also be helpful in making a report.

Report? What report?

I can hear you now. "What? We have to get official about this?" Well, yeah, we do. Because if we don't, your friend is going to continue to be abused or at the very least continue to hurt. So, take a big breath and let's talk about the "T" word.

## TELLING

If your friend has not told anyone else about the abuse, then you have just entered the trickiest part of being a friend to someone who's been sexually abused: to tell or not to tell.

Your friend may have sworn you to secrecy, may have told you that you can't breathe a word about this to anyone. The bottom line is this: you have to tell about the abuse. It is as simple and as difficult as that.

There are lots of good reasons for telling, but we're going to focus on the top three:

I. Your friend's safety

2. The law

3. Other potential victims

### YOUR FRIEND'S SAFETY

If the person who abused your friend has either died or moved far away, then your buddy is not in immediate danger. Maybe he's talking to you about the abuse because it's really bothering him or because he's worried that being a victim of sexual abuse means there's something wrong with him. You can reassure your friend and remind him that it wasn't his fault. But in the long run, the only thing that will really help your friend sort out all the junk that sexual abuse puts in a person's life is to talk to a professional who has expertise in handling sexual abuse. (How to find an individual like that is discussed on page 123.)

However, if the abuser is big brother, and Mom and Dad are going out of town and leaving big brother in charge for the weekend, then your friend is definitely at risk. Since there won't be a mom or dad around to "interrupt" things, it's possible that the abuse could get worse. Your friend may need some help to keep safe, which means you have to tell somebody about the abuse. This way the abuse can be stopped and your friend can be safe.

### THE LAW

Many states have laws about reporting sexual abuse. Some states have very specific laws and say that anybody who is an educator, police officer, medical person, or social worker must report all suspected abuse. Other states have more general laws that say *anybody* who suspects a child is being abused must report. Some states have both laws. Depending on what state you live in, you may, by law, be required to report the abuse.

### OTHER KIDS

People who sexually abuse kids do not always just stop abusing with one kid. Often the brothers and sisters of a victim are being abused, too—without the victim's knowing about it. A guy might think that by enduring the abuse and not telling, he's keeping his brothers and sisters safe. Wrong. There is a very good chance that his siblings are suffering in silence, too.

Sexual abuse can also go from one generation to another. A brother who sexually abuses his sister can grow up to be a father who sexually abuses his children. An aunt who sexually abuses her nephew can become a grandmother who sexually abuses her grandchildren. A coach, scout-leader, teacher, minister, doctor, or babysitter can have access to hundreds of kids who are all at risk. Look how many kids might suffer because no one had the guts to take a stand.

If you haven't convinced yourself that you need to report the abuse because of the law or because your friend is in danger, then think about all the other kids out there who are at risk because nobody will stand up and say, "Enough! This is not going to continue." So tell. Tell for your friend and tell for all the other kids out there who may be at risk.

### YOUR FRIEND'S REACTION

Okay, you understand the need to tell. You have thought it through and this is the only way you can see to help your friend. You or the adult you've talked to are going to make a report. It seems only fair to let your friend know you are going to do that. Your friend is most likely not going to think this is a great idea. In fact, there's a good chance that your friend could go ballistic.

Please understand that this person has suffered through the abuse because telling seems to be a fate worse than death. He is probably not going to jump for joy at the suggestion that his abuse be reported. He runs the risk that people will not believe him or that people will think the abuse was his fault. It will also mean bringing the sense of shame and guilt out into the open, having all his friends and neighbors know his business. It's also possible that the abuser has threatened him or people he loves with harm if he tells. Your friend has already taken a gigantic leap of faith by telling you. He is not going to be happy about the prospect of telling other people.

Give your friend some time to adjust. He may come to see that making a report is the only way the abuse will stop. He may continue to threaten you, swear at you, and take you off his party list. You'll have to stand firm and still report the abuse.

If you've already confided in an adult, you may want to consider telling that to your friend. Tell her that this adult can be an advocate for her. This adult can report the abuse to the authorities, possibly be present when she has to be interviewed by a social worker or detective, and be generally supportive.

Your friend may still resist and try to make you promise that you won't do anything about the situation. She may try to make you feel guilty that you are thinking about reporting the abuse. She may threaten you with all kinds of things: "I'll never speak to you again; I'll kill myself; I'll deny it" and on and on.

Stand firm. Let your friend know that you care too much about her to not do something about this. It won't be easy.

Your friend's concerns are legitimate. When sexual abuse is reported, the victim's life, the abuser's life, and their families' lives are never the same. And the change isn't always for the better.

But if you don't do something about it, who will? If people don't start taking a stand and saying, "My friend is really angry at me, but I know that I'm doing the right thing," then sexual abuse will continue forever and generations of kids will have to spend the rest of their lives trying to put the pieces back together just because nobody stood up for them.

## MAKING A REPORT

Making a report is simple. All you need to do is call the police and tell them you want to report child sexual abuse or call the operator and ask for the number of the department of social services for your county. Again, just say that you want to make a report of child sexual abuse and you will be connected with a child abuse worker or a "screener." You need to give the name of the victim (your friend) and his or her address or school. You need to give the name of the offender (the person who is abusing your friend) as well as his or her address—if you have it. If not, that's okay. One thing you need to keep in mind is that reports of abuse need to be made to the authorities in the county or city where the abuse occurred.

If your friend is being abused by his uncle who lives in a city fifty miles away and that's where the abuse occurred, you need to report it to the authorities in that city. If you don't know how to reach them, then make the report to *your* local authorities and they will either take it from there or help you make the report to the correct jurisdiction.

Once the report is made, your friend will be interviewed by a detective or social worker or both. And the whole judicial process will begin.

I'm not going to kid you. Our justice system is not the greatest when it comes to dealing effectively with sexual abuse, but there are people who are trying to make it better and who really care about the victim. My hope is that you and your friend will encounter some of these folks who can make the whole thing a bit easier.

## TAKING CARE OF YOU

 I told you at the beginning of this chapter that you were in for a bumpy ride. Being a friend to a person who's been sexually abused can seem like you're riding a roller coaster that has gone out of control. There may even be times when you feel the need to get off.

Part of the difficulty is simply dealing with the ups and downs your friend is going through. She may be happy, confident, and easygoing one day and a total basket case the next. You may find that around other people she's Ms. Got-it-all-together, but when the two of you are alone, she talks about suicide.

You may find that your relationship with her has changed, that you don't talk about everyday stuff anymore, that the only topic you discuss is the abuse, that your friend is like a drowning person and you are the life preserver. This can get old.

On the other hand, your friend may totally wipe you out of his life. No more party invitations, no more hanging around together, nothing. He may snub you in the halls and pretend that you don't exist. Worse, he may spread rumors and stories about you. None of this is easy to take—especially if you used to be good friends. Just try to understand that your buddy is coping the best way he knows how. It's not right or fair that you become the whipping-boy and the object of all the anger, but prepare yourself; it may happen.

(Right about now you're probably wishing that your friend had never told you anything, right?)

You need to take care of you. If the behavior gets too difficult to handle or the anger becomes more than you can deal with, take a break. Hang out with some other friends for a while. Cool off. But, and this is a big but, *do not* discuss the breakup of your friendship with anyone else. Other friends may ask you why you're not hanging around together anymore. You *do not* need to go into the details of why. "We're just taking a break from one another for a while" is plenty of answer. You *do* owe your friend privacy on this subject among your friends. If she wants to tell other friends about the abuse, that's *her* right.

The one exception to this rule of not telling anyone else about the abuse is the trusted adult you have decided to tell. Even though you may have to take that step in spite of your friend's objections, you are not invading his privacy or trying to wreck his reputation. In fact, what you're doing is trying to save his life. Be smart about talking to other people; preserve your friend's privacy but not at the expense of his well-being.

## DEALING WITH THE CHANGES IN YOUR FRIEND

One of the hardest things for you may be to watch your friend change. She may start dressing or acting differently. She may get involved with drugs or alcohol or she may start "putting out" for guys. Maybe she'll drop out of sports or clubs or her grades may crash. Lots of things may start to look and be different about your friend and it may be really tough to see her taking a downward slide.

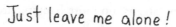

It's hard to watch your friend change.

The important thing to remember is that you may or may not be able to do something about that. You can try talking to your friend and letting her know that you really care about her, that you're concerned about the changes you see. But be prepared; she may get angry with you and tell you to mind your own business. Or she may just quietly cut you out of her life. This can hurt.

It's important to remember that your friend is really confused, scared, and hurting. I know it's not a lot of comfort when you're up against anger, resentment, and snubs. But that is the fact—your friend is really struggling. You may or may not be able to stick with him through the struggle. Try to stay in touch with how *you* are doing.

If things are getting too rough, it's not wrong to pull away from your friend. Just be sure your friend knows it's because you can't take the harassment anymore and not that you're embarrassed to be his friend because he was sexually abused. You could say something like, "This is obviously a really hard thing for you or anyone to deal with. I just need to take a break for a while because it's getting pretty intense. I still care about you and will always be here if you need me." That lets your friend know that you're still a friend but *you* need a break and will be back when you're rested up.

It can be very painful to watch a friend change, take a nosedive, or fall apart. It can be even more painful when you know that you can't do anything about it. I mean, how old are you? Thirteen? Seventeen? Nineteen? Do you have a degree in counseling, psychiatry, or psychology? Do you have experience helping people sort through the trauma of sexual abuse? Of course not. You are simply a teenager who's trying his or her best to be a good friend to a person who's hurting big-time. So go easy on yourself. If your friend runs away from home, it's not your fault. If your friend gets in trouble with the police, it's not your fault. If your friend tries suicide, it's not your fault. None of this is your fault. Just be a friend to the best of your ability.

## ANSWERS FROM FRIENDS OF SEXUALLY ABUSED KIDS

*What should a friend do when someone tells her he has been sexually abused?*

I think she shouldn't keep it to herself. She should tell somebody else.

*Should a friend tell the victim that he's going to tell someone?*

I didn't. I was too scared of what she'd do to me. My mother was the trusted adult I got involved. And she made the report.

*What else should a friend do or not do?*

Don't ask about specifics, no matter how much you want to know to make sure about what happened. I really think he needs to tell you that in his own time, and only if he wants to. I'm afraid if I had asked him about anything specific, he would have shut up altogether. . . . It's also important to say you believe him.

*What is it like to be a friend to someone who's been sexually abused?*

It's hard. . . . I realized that Paul (the victim) had a lot of garbage in his life so he gave a lot of the garbage to me. But that didn't always make it easy. . . . You're only a kid; how can you expect to take all this? At the same time I felt there was sort of a responsibility in being his friend, to support him.

*Knowing that an adult you told would go to social services and make a report, would you still tell?*

Yes. Because I think that is the only way that victims . . . will ever really get help or get through it. At the same time, you're helping yourself. I would really have felt responsible if she had done anything to herself and I hadn't told anyone else or tried anything else.

*What other advice do you have for friends?*

It's important to realize that you can't solve all the problems. There are other qualified people, capable people who can help out. Don't try to help your friend alone.

## DO THE BEST YOU CAN

Keep in mind that this is not a competition or a test with grades. This is simply about being a friend, caring about someone, trying to help, making sure *you* don't go nuts in the process. Give it your best shot and then let it be.

## I Will Be Your Friend

The tears start flowing from your eyes

You try to be so strong

But deep inside you ask yourself,

"Where did I go wrong?"


Your life is like an hourglass

Dropping grains of sand

And I watch from the outside

To find out where they land


To say I understand your pain

Would simply be a lie

And maybe I never will

But I promise I will try

Dark shadows are fading fast

Of innocence lost in the past

They say time heals all wounds

Who knows better than you?

As you feel your heart begin to mend

Just know that I will be your friend

# 15

# What Some Survivors Would Like You to Know

I U you to three terrific people. Each of these young people is a survivor of sexual abuse. Their situations are all different, but they have many things in common: the issues they are struggling to deal with, the feelings that occasionally overwhelm them, and the fact that each was robbed of a childhood. I hope you see something of yourself in their honesty, courage, and determination to heal from the injury sexual abuse has inflicted on their lives.

## JENNIFER

When you first meet Jennifer, you're not surprised to learn that she was once a cheerleader. She has an all-American girl look about her: clear skin, hazel eyes, and shiny brown hair. From the outside, her family also has the all-American look. Jennifer and her mother were active in the local church—singing in the choir, ringing handbells. Jennifer's dad worked long hours and was seen in the community as a hard-working guy who was a good provider for his family.

A different picture begins to emerge as Jennifer tells what her family was really like.

> My father began abusing me when I was about three, at least that's my first memory of abuse. For a long time I thought this was a normal thing because I didn't know any

different. Then when I was twelve, he began having sex with me and it really started hitting me that something wasn't right.

I tried to tell my mother. I told her at least three or four times in the whole eleven years of abuse. She would say something to him and he would stop for a week. He would be mad at me for a couple of days and wouldn't talk to me or anything. Then it would just start up again.

I remember the first time I ever told her was when I was about five. I saw a *Playboy* magazine at my best friend's house. Some guy was laying on top of a girl in one of the pictures. My mother was there and we showed it to her and my friend's mother. Then later, when we got home, I said to my mother, "Ma, do you remember what them people were doing on the front of the magazine? Well that's what Daddy's doing to me." I remember that's exactly how I told her.

Yeah, my mother was pretty dumb about it, too!

After that, she would ask me once in a while, "Is your father still doing that to you?" Most of the time I would tell her no. When she would ask my father about it, he would say I was hearing it from school or my friends or whatever.

People say, "Why didn't you tell someone else?" But I couldn't. I was so afraid that my family would break up and I'd have to go to a foster home. That's what happened on the TV shows. You know, those after-school specials where a little girl would get put out of the family and she wouldn't be able to see her mother. Plus my father would tell me stuff when I was little like if I told anybody they wouldn't believe me or if I told my mother she was going to be mad at me.

Everything came to a head when I was fourteen. It was a Saturday. I don't know what made me tell; I think I just got frustrated or whatever. I was in my room fixing my hair and my father came in and just started touching on me and stuff. I said, "Stop. Get off of me." Then he grabbed me on my bed and I kept saying, "Get off of me, get off of me." But he wouldn't.

Somehow I managed to push him off. I was just so mad. I started crying and ran out of the house. I ran all the way over to my girlfriend's house—about one mile—I ran the whole way. I told my girlfriend's mother and father what had happened and then waited 'til my mom got home. I called her, and she came over to my girlfriend's house and we sat down and talked.

At first, my mother said, "Do you want me to get your father some counseling? Why don't we just get him counseling?" And I said, "No! I want the police in on it. If you don't call the police, I'm going to go to school on Monday and tell my guidance counselor."

By the time we got home that night, my father was already asleep. My mother left him a note and told him what I had told her. Then we went to bed. I couldn't sleep all night. I was awake when he got up in the morning. I heard him rip open the note, read it, and then crumple it up and throw it in the fire. He took some money my mom had been saving and left. We didn't know if he would come back or not.

My mother took me to see a therapist on Monday, then on Tuesday, a social worker and a police detective came to school to interview me. After that, I had to go into a foster home because no one knew if my father would be coming back, and if he did, what he would do. It wasn't too bad, though. My friend's parents were foster parents and I stayed with them. I also got to see my mom every day.

About a week later, my father came back and turned himself in. At first he was denying that he did anything. Then they played the tape for him that they had made when they interviewed me. He finally admitted to everything and said he didn't want me to have to get up on the stand and have to testify. He also told them he was feeling suicidal and had been thinking of ways to kill himself during the past week.

My brother denied it, too.

The police sent him for a psychiatric evaluation and he was admitted to the hospital for a couple of weeks. After that he went to jail for a couple of weeks. But then my mom bailed him out. I was a little bit mad at her for doing that. I wanted him to be in jail. But I understood why she did it. My father pays a lot of our bills and if he didn't work, we wouldn't have any financial support.

He wasn't allowed to have any contact with me. We did talk once on the phone, but that was by accident. I told him I was sorry. I started crying and everything. I felt so bad about all the trouble I had caused.

But then I took it back. During our first responsibility session, I said, "I take back the sorry I told you, because I'm not sorry now."

Jennifer's grades dropped after the disclosure and she eventually was kicked off the cheerleading squad. She had a hard time keeping up in school because so much of her energy was being focused on dealing with going to court, therapy, having no contact with her father, and adjusting to the changes in her relationship with her mother. She became suicidal and was admitted to the hospital for a brief stay. Jennifer says now that without counseling, she would never have made it.

Jennifer didn't have face-to-face contact with her father for two years. They would see each other across a parking lot or pass each other in the waiting room on therapy nights; but they didn't speak or interact. This was really hard for Jennifer and she often went home in tears, feeling a mixture of sadness and guilt and grief.

After two years of hard work on her part as well as her father's, Jennifer and her dad met for a responsibility session (for more on responsibility sessions, see page 217). Jennifer wrote down everything she wanted to say in case she got nervous and blanked out. The first session was the hardest—partly because she felt nervous about seeing her father after so long and partly because she had some tough questions to ask him.

> My father had never told me why he and his first wife had gotten divorced. I had this idea stuck in my head that he probably abused his other daughter, too. He says no. Then I asked him about being arrested when I was three for molesting my cousin. He said the abuse never happened.
>
> I think he did it. I wouldn't be surprised because there used to be a girl who lived across the street who would babysit me. My father would always have her and her friends sit on his lap and stuff. I saw her some time after I told about the abuse and she told me how my father used to flirt with her and stuff.

It's very important to Jennifer to have a relationship with her father. She says she trusts him, but she seems to have reservations. He still tries to control her through "father type" statements ("Don't stay out too late. Are you wearing a warm coat? Where will you be?"). And he sometimes tries to play Jennifer against her mother. But for the most part, Jennifer feels good about their relationship.

> I believe he's sincere. He's just the type of person that nags. It still feels good because he's starting to be like a father to me now. Before, he acted like my boyfriend. I don't really mind him nagging me about school and everything because that's what fathers are supposed to do.

Jennifer's relationship with her mother has also changed for the better. The first year and a half after Jennifer's disclosure was particularly rough.

> We fought a lot. I just had a lot of anger inside of me that I took out on her because she was the first person there. And my mother had a lot of anger inside too. She always yelled so she has had to work on talking to me without yelling. Right after I told about the abuse, she was too much my mother. Then for a while she was trying to be more my friend than my mother. Now I think she's just where she needs to be. I like it just like this.

Jennifer again credits therapy for the good relationship she shares with her mom. They are still in counseling every other week and feel very comfortable with that.

Now that she's seventeen, Jennifer is making plans for her future. She intends to get her GED and then finish up her cosmetology course. She would like to be an aesthetician giving facials, performing electrolysis. Her eyes sparkle as she talks about her hopes for the future.

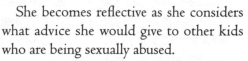

Yeah, me too!

She becomes reflective as she considers what advice she would give to other kids who are being sexually abused.

> I used to think I was the only person in the world going through this. It's just now hitting me that there are still other little girls in this world who are having the same experience. I wish I could go out and help them. I wish I could get to all of them and ask them to tell somebody because they don't have to go through it.
>
> Even though telling might mean having to go to foster care or seeing somebody you care about go to jail, you still should tell. You

might go through a little bit of pain, but it's worth it in the long run.

---

## DANIEL

I met Daniel through a lecture I gave to some college students. He's a good-looking young man of twenty—not very tall, but solidly built —and looks like the athlete he is.

It was obvious, as we talked, that Daniel's memories still hurt him a lot. He found it difficult to talk about the specifics of the abuse, but he was generous with telling me his feelings about it.

> I come from a, well, I guess you'd have to say wealthy family. I have an older brother and an older sister. We used to be a tightly knit family when we were younger, but things seemed to fall apart as each of us hit our teens.
>
> When I was fifteen, my brother developed some serious mental illnesses that got worse when he went to college and my sister was into some big-time rebellion. My father was real wrapped up in my brother and my mother was real wrapped up in my sister and there wasn't anybody around for me. I started getting into serious, serious drugs and alcohol. I figured if I drink then I can be an adult, and if I'm an adult, I can deal with anything.

By the time Dan was sixteen, he was in a lot of trouble. He was flunking school, drunk all the time, and beginning to self-abuse (he and two of his friends would make up new ways to hurt themselves). As Dan puts it, "I was the type of kid who if your daughter brought me home, you would not be very happy. I did not look good. I wasn't taking care of myself, and I was drinking a lot." At this point, Daniel had no concrete memories of being abused. He would occasionally have "flashes" but nothing he could figure out and say for certain, "I was abused."

Dan was hospitalized by his parents after he tried to commit suicide. At first he hated the hospital, "The first three days really sucked." But after two months, he had managed to kick his drug and alcohol habit and had begun to feel better about himself. About three days before leaving the hospital, Dan had a major flashback of abuse by a camp counselor.

I really didn't remember that much. I mean, I remember scenes, but I really don't know how long it happened. I see like scenes out in a field or scenes in a bunk or something, but it's not complete.

My memories are fuzzy, too!

He decided not to tell anyone at the hospital because he was afraid he would have to stay longer. So he left the hospital trying to ignore the memories that were beginning to erupt, and to just get on with his life. This worked for about a year or so. Then, when Dan was eighteen, his world began to fall apart again.

I was seeing a psychiatrist. My family was a mess and I really wanted to try to work some things out. So I asked my sister to come with me to one of my meetings with the doctor. It was the summer I was eighteen and during the session she said, "Danny, don't you remember when we were kids?" and I'm like, "What are you talking about?" So she started telling the doctor what she had done to me when I was eight and she was ten. It was some very sick stuff. And all the memories started flashing back in front of me and ugh! It killed me, you know? It hurts. It sucks. I mean, my own sister.

Daniel found therapy to be his lifeline after his memories began returning. He had the memories of his sister's abuse to deal with as well as the memories of the camp counselor's abuse. Today Daniel struggles with his relationship with his sister as well as his sexuality.

His sister, he says, knows how to push all of his buttons and make him "very, very mad." He hates her life-style, the power she has over him and his parents as well as her disregard for other people's feelings. He finds it difficult to be with her and not remember the abuse.

> How can one of your family members do something like that to you? Your own family member trying to have sex with you. It doesn't make you feel clean. Dirty isn't the word I'm looking for. But it doesn't make you feel. . . . I don't know, incest is such an ugly word.

Daniel also blames his sister for "the way I act toward women. The way it's manifested itself is just crazy, absolutely ludicrous."

> I can't stay in a long-term relationship with a woman. I remember my sophomore year of high school; I went through twenty-five girls in three weeks. I just can't stay with one woman.
>
> I dated one girl for two years but that's mostly because she was really into the relationship. There were times when I literally hated her, didn't want to be with her. Sometimes she would do things that would remind me of my sister and I would have to get out of there.

Daniel wrestles with his own sexuality. He occasionally worries that he might be gay.

> I think it's normal for most males to question their sexuality at some time in their life. Mine was a little bit more intense. My doctor's been real helpful in sorting this out. He keeps telling me that it wasn't my fault and any feelings I had back then (during the abuse) are not the feelings I have to have today. But I would never tell another male about being sexually abused by a male. It makes me nervous. It would be too hard to do.

Daniel also struggles with his views of women and sex.

> The thing is, I've really never truly enjoyed sex. I mean it's fun, yeah, it's great, but there's got to be more to it. I

mean after the first ten or fifteen minutes, I'm kinda like, "This is not fun" and I'm thinking about everything and anything just to get done. I don't know where the emotional part of sex is. I'm looking for it, waiting for it.

I know about this.

I'm a very physical guy. I play a lot of sports, wrestle, am a black belt in karate. I've been brought up to be very physical. Every now and then if I'm having sex with some girl and I'm not enjoying it, which is the majority of the time, I usually start thinking, you know, how easy it would be just to destroy this person. It'd be so easy to kill this person or so easy to put this person in pain. I've talked to my doctor about it, but it's still something I need to work on.

Daniel hopes to one day get married and have children. He feels very sure that he will never abuse his own children. He believes that survivors should tell their marital partners and even their girlfriends before marriage about the abuse.

I think it's important in any relationship for a partner to know because sometimes I may have a flash of my sister and start to freak and I'd want my partner to at least understand.

I've lost track of Daniel since I interviewed him. Last I heard, he had left college and was back home with his family. I hope he's keeping well. This is what he asked me to tell other kids who have been sexually abused.

You're gonna be okay. Don't let it destroy you. If you destroy yourself because of this person [the abuser] then you've lost the battle. But if you're able to move on and deal with the feelings, then you've beat it, you've beat him or her. You're gonna be a much stronger person because you survived it.

---

## JULIA

Confident. That's the word that describes Julia. At eighteen, she has the height and slenderness of a model, dark eyes, dark hair, and the kind of skin the word "alabaster" was invented for. Julia also has a certain presence about her. She seems very composed and mature as we sit in the living room of her mother's home while her ten-month-old daughter naps upstairs.

Julia has memories of not only sexual abuse, but physical and psychological abuse as well. She remembers being hung in a closet by handcuffs, being forced to read books on Satanism, being threatened with death of herself or her firstborn, and other acts perpetrated for the purpose of scaring her enough to ensure her silence.

Her first memory of abuse is when she was three. She's not sure how long it continued because her next memories are of when she was eleven or twelve. Her biological father was the abuser except for one episode she recalls from when she was around thirteen.

My father took me to his office and I remember he and another man who worked with him abused me together. But I kept trying to repress the memories. I'd tell myself I wasn't remembering right, I was crazy, I was making it up— because this was my father and a friend of the family.

Julia's family is a portrait of what *dysfunctional* means. Her father ruled the family through physical abuse, verbal abuse, and mind games. Her mother came to believe that she was nothing and that she deserved her husband's physical and emotional abuse. Her older brother was kept in line by being beaten with two-by-fours until he would beg for his father to stop. Her older sister was told she was a whore and a slut and constantly accused of letting boys sneak into her bedroom. Julia's younger sisters were threatened with beatings, having their heads pushed into the toilet, or being forced to read Satanic material that talked about how to murder children.

I came from a perfect family, too.

On the outside, Julia's family appeared to be a model Christian family. They went to church regularly. In fact Julia's father was part of the ruling body of the church and taught Sunday School and Bible study classes. They didn't have a television for the first thirteen years of Julia's life. Instead, they would do "family" things like play board games or take nature walks. Like I said, a model family. But when you peel back the layers, a totally different picture begins to emerge.

My mother first left my father when I was about seven or eight. I think it was because he had hit her. All I remember is when she told us we were going back. I sobbed all night in my bed. I didn't want to go back.

The second time she left him, I was about twelve. That time it was because he was acting so crazy. He wasn't sleeping. All he did was pace back and forth, back and forth and my mom was scared. So we left.

The third time she left him, I was fourteen and had just made my third suicide attempt. My mother didn't know I had been molested but she knew that things were not all right. So we left again. My mom never went back after that.

Julia made three suicide attempts in three months. Each time, she hoped that someone would be able to help her. The first time, she hoped her mother would do something. The second time, she hoped someone at school would help her. The third time, she called a suicide hot line and the counselor sent an ambulance to her home since she had already cut her wrists. It was after this attempt that Julia was admitted to a psychiatric hospital.

I was placed on a family therapy unit which meant I never had therapy with a psychiatrist by myself. When you're always with your family, you're not going to say anything. So basically it was a joke. The abuse never got talked about, and I got released after a month.

After Julia left the hospital, she went to live with her mother and a younger sister who had moved out of the family home while she was hospitalized. Things were tough. Julia was constantly fighting a battle of depression and feelings of craziness as well as developing panic attacks. She was also trying to adjust to a mother who was now standing up for herself and laying down some rules.

It was really hard. We were living in this dump of a place; I missed my littlest sister and we didn't have any money. All I could think about was, "If I were living with Dad right now, I could have nice clothes, my own room back, all my own stuff." I couldn't cope.

Over the next year or so, Julia went back and forth between her parents' homes. Part of it was her own willfulness; part of it was the difficulty of living away from the family home and her sister and her friends; and part of it was the stupidity of the courts in giving her father custody of all the children.

During the six or seven months that she lived with her father between the ages of fifteen and sixteen, Julia began sleeping around, drinking, staying out late, skipping school, and generally going down the drain. After a particularly bad episode of physical abuse, Julia decided she needed to get away from her father and went once again to live with her mother.

It was terrible. I didn't want to listen to her or pay attention to her rules. I had a lot of anger at her for not doing anything to protect me and my sisters and brother. Sometimes I blamed her more than my father because I knew that my father was sick and she wasn't. So why couldn't she see it? It's like, "I know he's sick, but you're not sick so why didn't you do something?"

I blamed my mother, too.

Julia and her mother did manage to begin a new relationship based on mutual understanding and commitment to working through problems. One morning, not long after she had moved back in with her mother, Julia refused to get up to go to school. Her mother said, "Fine. You don't want to go to high school? No problem. You can go to college." And that day, at the age of sixteen, Julia enrolled at the local community college where she continues to work on a degree in psychology.

This would seem like a good place to end—on this happily-ever-after note. But that's not real life. When she was seventeen-and-a-half, Julia was date raped. Just as her physical injuries were beginning to heal, she learned she was pregnant. She decided to go through with the pregnancy and keep the baby. Her daughter is a beautiful, happy child. Her decision is not without its burdens, though. Julia is on welfare, attending school on loans that will have to be paid back, living under her mother's roof, trying to deal with being a teen mom, working on the scars the sexual abuse has left on her soul, and learning to feel good about herself again.

I have problems with some things, like sometimes I'll doubt—did it really happen? Sometimes I feel so crazy. I sometimes worry that maybe I'm not lovable or something because nobody helped me when I was trying so hard to get their attention.

I have a tremendous fear about losing my daughter because of my own custody battles I went through as a child with my family. I mean, I walked into the court once with my arm in a sling from my father's wrenching it behind my back, and the judge said it was irrelevant. The social workers presented my information about being sexually abused and the possibility that my sister had been sexually abused and they still sent us back to my father.

I know I'm a good parent. I nurse her, I clothe her, I never yell at her. I think I'm the best mother I can be. But I'm still scared that somehow, somebody's going to take my daughter from me. I worry that I'll have a panic attack and be paralyzed and she'll get hurt. I feel that I'm being watched by the people who know I've been a victim of sexual abuse—will she screw up? Is she going to do something wrong?

Julia, however, refuses to allow other people to run her life. She deals with her fears as well as she can and is involved in therapy whenever there is enough money to pay for a session. She is very clear about what she will tolerate from others and what she will not and has a strong future plan mapped out.

I really want to help kids as much as I can to work through their problems. I want to help the kids who have gotten to the breaking point and who need help right then. So many times I've been there myself and there wasn't anyone around to help. I want to be the one to help other kids.

I don't think there are any pat answers and "everything's going to be okay" isn't always helpful. I guess the biggest thing that has helped me is a combination of two things: (1) to understand that the abuse was not my fault, and (2) to know that I don't have to explain myself. The way I see it, once you find you can stop explaining yourself, you stop feeling responsible.

## CINDI

If it's true that courage is the measurement of what we have endured, then these are three of the most courageous people I know. The one common theme I have seen running through the life of every survivor I talk to is courage. It is probably a theme in your life also; you just may not have recognized it yet.

As I finish the last draft of this book, I am aware that I haven't specifically answered the question asked in the title, "How Long Does It Hurt?" Well, today is December 22, 1993, three days before Christmas and I am painfully aware that once again I will spend Christmas without my family of origin—without my mother and father, my brothers and sister, nieces, cousins. I hasten to add that that is because of decisions I felt I had to make to survive. However, it still hurts.

How long does it hurt? I guess the honest answer is, forever; but the hurt is no longer a

Cindi ... We have a surprise for you!

searing of my soul. It no longer has the power to bring me to the edge of suicide or the depths of depression. The hurt no longer fills my life. It can't—because too much grace and mercy have brought healing to my wounds and my pain.

I will spend this Christmas with a man who has loved me faithfully for over seventeen years, two incredibly healthy, bright, and delightful sons, and a circle of people who have become my family through marriage and friendship.

I have come a far distance since that long ago summer night of my seventeenth year, when I said, "Mom, I have something to tell you and if you don't believe me, I don't know what I'll do." In the past twenty-some years I have learned that I have value, worth, rights, and the ability to say "no." I have come to understand that love does not have to be a weapon and healing is an ongoing process.

So, even though the hurt may never disappear, it does get smaller, more manageable. It doesn't happen by magic. It requires you first to acknowledge that you were hurt, then to tell that you were hurt, then to decide to move on from the hurt. But if you've gotten this far in the book, you know that.

Doing it is another thing.

However, if you take these steps, you'll find that the hurt will eventually diminish. And in its place, there will be a space in your life where healing, love, friendship, and grace can pour in and make you whole. I know this for a fact. I have been where you have been. I hope this book helps you to travel a far distance in your own healing—a far distance to a place where the hurt is merely a scratch and the joy is like the sun warming your life.

You guys are terrific!

# Bibliography

Adams-Tucker, Christine. "The Unmet Psychiatric Needs of Sexually Abused Youths: Referrals from a Child Protection Agency and Clinical Evaluations." *Journal of the American Academy of Child Psychiatry,* Vol. 23 (1984), pp. 6:659-667

Bass, Ellen, and Davis, Laura. *The Courage to Heal.* New York: Harper-Collins, 1988

Bell, Ruth and Associates. *Changing Bodies, Changing Lives.* New York: Vintage Books, 1988

Blume, E. Sue. *Secret Survivors.* New York: John Wiley & Sons, 1990

Bradshaw, John. *Bradshaw on the Family.* Deerfield Beach, FL: Health Communications, Inc., 1988

Burgess, Ann W.; Hartman, Carol R.; McCormack, Arlene. "Abused to Abuser: Antecedents of Socially Deviant Behaviors." *American Journal Psychiatry,* Vol. 144 (1987), pp. 1431-1436

Burgess, Ann Wolbert; Groth, Nicholas A.; Holmstrom, Lynda Lytle; Sgroi, Suzanne M. *Sexual Assault of Children and Adolescents.* Lexington, KY: Lexington Books, 1978

Butler, Sandra. *Conspiracy of Silence.* San Francisco: Volcano Press, Inc., 1985

Byerly, Carolyn. *The Mother's Book.* Dubuque, IA: Kendall/Hunt Publishing Co., 1985

Cooper, Burton Z. *Why God?* Atlanta: John Knox Press, 1988

Courtois, Christine A. *Healing the Incest Wound.* New York: W.W. Norton & Co., 1988

Crewdson, John. *By Silence Betrayed.* New York: HarperCollins, 1988

Davis, Laura. *Allies in Healing.* New York: Harper Perennial, 1991

DiBlasio, Frederick A. "The Role of Social Workers' Religious Beliefs in Helping Family Members Forgive." *Families In Society: The Journal of Contemporary Human Services,* Vol. 74 (1993), 163-170.

DiBlasio, Fredrick A. and Benda, Brent B. "Practitioners, Religion, and the Use of Forgiveness in the Clinical Setting." *Psychotherapy and Religious Values.* E. L. Worthington, Jr., Editor. Grand Rapids, MI: Baker Book House, 1993

Donaldson, Mary Ann. *Incest Years After.* Fargo, ND: The Village Family Service Center, 1983

Donnelly, Doris. *Putting Fogiveness Into Practice.* Allen, TX: Argus Communications, 1982

Dziech, Billie Wright and Schudson, Charles B. *On Trial—America's Courts and Their Treatment of Sexually Abused Children.* 2nd edition. Boston: Beacon Press, 1991

Engel, Beverly. *The Right to Innocence.* New York: Ivy Books, 1989

Engel, Beverly. *Divorcing a Parent.* New York: Fawcett Columbine, 1990

Estes, Clariss Pinkola, Ph.D. *Women Who Run With the Wolves.* New York: Ballentine Books, 1993

Fay, Jennifer J. and Flerchinger, Billie Jo & Associates. *Top Secret.* Renton, WA: King Co. Sexual Assault Resource Center, 1988

Finkelhor, David and Associates. *A Sourcebook on Child Sexual Abuse.* Newbury Park, CA: Sage Publications, 1986

Finkelhor, David. *Sexually Victimized Children.* New York: The Free Press, 1981

Forward, Susan and Buck, Craig. *Betrayal of Innocence.* New York: Penguin Books, 1987

Fraser, Sylvia. *My Father's House.* New York: HarperCollins, 1989

Gil, Eliana. *United We Stand.* Walnut Creek, CA: Launch Press, 1990.

Grubman-Black, Stephen D. *Broken Boys/Mending Men.* Blue Ridge Summit, PA: TAB Books, 1990

Hancock, Maxine and Mains, Karen Burton. *Child Sexual Abuse: A Hope for Healing.* Wheaton, IL: Harold Shaw Publishers, 1987

Herman, Judith. *Father-Daughter Incest.* Cambridge, MA: Harvard University Press, 1981

Horton, Anne L. and Williamson, Judith A. *Abuse and Religion.* Lexington, KY: Lexington Books, 1988

Hunter, Mic. *Abused Boys.* New York: Fawcett Columbine, 1990

Hynes, Angela. *Puberty: An Illustrated Manual for Parents & Daughters.* New York: TOR Books, 1989

Jarvis-Kirkendall, Carol and Jeffery Kirkendall. *Without Consent.* Scottsdale, AZ: Swan Press, Inc., 1989

Kaplan, Sandra J. and Zitrin, Arthur. "Case Assessment by Child Protective Services." *Journal of the American Academy of Child Psychiatry,* Vol. 22 (1983), pp. 3:253-256

Krener, Penelope. "After Incest: Secondary Prevention?" *Journal of the American Academy of Child Psychiatry,* Vol. 24 (1985), pp. 2:231-234

Lew, Mike. *Victims No Longer.* New York: HarperCollins, 1988

Madaras, Lynda. *The What's Happening To My Body Book for Girls.* New York: Newmarket Press, 1988

Madaras, Lynda. *The What's Happening To My Body Book for Boys.* New York: Newmarket Press, 1988

Maltz, Wendy and Holman, Beverly. *Incest and Sexuality.* Lexington, KY: Lexington Books, 1987

Meiselman, Karin C. *Incest.* San Francisco: Jossey-Bass Publishers, 1986

Peters, David B. *A Betrayal of Innocence.* Dallas: Word Publishing, 1986

Pomeroy, Wardell B. *Girls and Sex.* New York: Dell Publishing Co., 1981

Pomeroy, Wardell B. *Boys and Sex.* New York: Dell Publishing Co., 1981

Poston, Carol and Lison, Karen. *Reclaiming Our Lives.* Boston: Little, Brown & Co., 1989

Rush, Florence. *The Best Kept Secret.* New York: McGraw-Hill Book Co., 1980

Russell, Diana E.H. *The Secret Trauma.* New York: Basic Books, Inc., 1986

Scarf, Maggie. *Intimate Partners.* New York, Ballantine Books, 1987

Seghorn, Theoharis K.; Prentky, Robert A.; Boucher, Richard J. "Childhood Sexual Abuse in the Lives of Sexually Aggressive

Offenders." *Journal American Academy Child Adolescent Psychiatry*, Vol. 26 (1987), pp. 2:262-267

Sgroi, Suzanne M., ed. Handbook of Clinical Intervention in Child Sexual Abuse. Lexington, KY: Lexington Books, 1982

Smedes, Lewis B. *Forgive & Forget—Healing the Hurts We Don't Deserve.* New York: Pocket Books, 1986

Thomas, T. *Men Surviving Incest.* Walnut Creek, CA: Launch Press, 1989

Tower, Cynthia Crosson. *Secret Scars.* New York: Penguin Books, 1989

Watkins, Jim. *Sex Is Not a Four-Letter Word.* Wheaton, IL: Tyndale House Publishers, Inc., 1991

Wilson, Sandra D. *Released from Shame.* Downers Grove, IL: Intervarsity Press, 1990

Woititz, Janet G. *Healing Your Sexual Self.* Deerfield Beach, FL: Health Communications, Inc., 1989

Wolter, Dwight Lee. *Forgiving Our Parents.* Minneapolis: Comp Care Publishers, 1989

Worthington, Everett L., Jr., and DiBlasio, Frederick A. "Promoting Mutual Forgiveness Within the Fractured Relationship." *Psychotherapy*, Vol. 27 (1990): 219-223

Wyatt, Gail Elizabeth and Powell, Gloria Johnson, eds. *Lasting Effects of Child Sexual Abuse.* Newbury Park, CA: Sage Publications, 1988

# Index

# The Authors

CYNTHIA L. MATHER is herself a survivor who brings to this book a firsthand knowledge of the issues facing victims of sexual abuse and incest. She has spent many years studying the literature; interviewing sexually abused teenagers and their friends and families; doing field research with judges, therapists, prosecutors, social workers, and offenders; and speaking at high schools, colleges, and churches. For these efforts, she won the 1992 Woman of the Year award from the Baltimore County Government Commission for Women. She is coeditor of *SOLOS II* and *SOLOS III*, anthologies of writings by survivors of sexual abuse and incest published by VOICES in Action, Inc.

KRISTINA E. DEBYE, LCSW-C, ACSW, DCSW, is coordinator of one of the leading sexual abuse treatment programs in the country. The program uses an integrated interdisciplinary approach to investigating sexual abuse cases and providing long-term multimodal therapy to incest families. Under her leadership, the program has expanded in size and scope and has received both local and national recognition.

Debye is a frequent lecturer on the impact of sexual abuse on the victim, the family, and the community. She also maintains a limited private practice in Towson, Maryland.